T0115670

THE LION TRACKER'S
GUIDE TO LIFE

ALSO BY BOYD VARTY

Cathedral of the Wild

THE
LION
TRACKER'S
GUIDE
TO LIFE

___

BOYD VARTY

Illustrations by Roxy Burrough

Houghton Mifflin Harcourt

Boston   New York

2019

Copyright © 2019 by Boyd Varty
Illustrations by Roxy Burrough © 2019 by Houghton Mifflin Harcourt

All rights reserved

For information about permission to reproduce selections from this book, write
to trade.permissions@hmhco.com or to Permissions, Houghton Mifflin Harcourt
Publishing Company, 3 Park Avenue, 19th Floor, New York, New York 10016.

www.hmhbooks.com

Library of Congress Cataloging-in-Publication Data
Names: Varty, Boyd, author. | Burrough, Roxy, illustrator.
Title: The lion tracker's guide to life / Boyd Varty ;
illustrations by Roxy Burrough.
Description: Boston : Houghton Mifflin Harcourt, 2019.
Identifiers: LCCN 2019002731 (print) | LCCN 2019003935 (ebook) |
ISBN 9780358100492 (ebook) | ISBN 9780358099772 (hardcover) |
ISBN 9780358172154 (audio)
Subjects: LCSH: Varty, Boyd. | Londolozi Game Reserve (South Africa) |
Lion hunting — South Africa — Londolozi Game Reserve. | Tracking
and trailing — South Africa — Londolozi Game Reserve. | Wildlife
conservation — South Africa — Londolozi Game Reserve.
Classification: LCC SK575.S5 (ebook) | LCC SK575.S5 V375 2019 (print) |
DDC 639.97/9757 — dc23
LC record available at https://lccn.loc.gov/2019002731

Book design by Emily Snyder

Printed in the United States of America
23 24 25 26 27 LBC 9 8 7 6 5

For my father, who has mentored so many

———

There are many varieties and specializations among shamans, but generically they were called Ajcuna, signifying "he or she who tracks it."

—MARTÍN PRECHTEL,
Secrets of the Talking Jaguar

CONTENTS

ACKNOWLEDGMENTS

It takes a village. This book has been the culmination of many years living on the track of my own life. I have spent a lot of time outside the conventional paths on trails of my own making. While this is a beautifully rewarding path, it can be lonely and it will put you face-to-face with your own doubts. I would not be able to live as a tracker without the incredible support I have received from my family, extended family, and village.

I thank my mother and father for always being an example of making their own path and for endless love and support. My sister, Bronwyn Varty Laburn, has been one of my greatest teachers, and her guidance has allowed me to keep moving forward. My brother-in-law, Richard Laburn, was a critical support in the early phases of the book and continues to be.

Martha Beck provided so much of my education as an

inner tracker and I will always be profoundly grateful for the gifts she has given me, including the ongoing encouragement to write and to follow my inner track.

To the shaman who apprenticed me: thank you.

I thank Tamara Day Shriver and Harry Kalmer for their assistance in creating this work as readers, curators, and fellow storytellers.

Koelle Simpson has been a true friend and encouraged me in living the ideas shared between these pages.

I am deeply grateful to Betsy Rapoport for her unwavering support and willingness to help me get my ideas out, as well as for always welcoming me as a weary traveler to her home.

A deep word of thanks to Tess Beasley and Maureen Chiquet, who have given me incredible assistance and provided the sanctuary that has allowed me to live with many unknowns.

I thank Tina Bennett, my agent, for the incredible guidance she provides as a reader, friend, and guide in the world of publishing. Thanks for taking a chance on me early on.

I am grateful to Lisa White, my editor at Houghton Mifflin Harcourt, for helping me shape this text.

I thank the owners of Londolozi Game Reserve for being custodians of a unique and sacred place. Londolozi is the home of the restoration, and it would not have been born or fostered without the wisdom of Allan Taylor, John Varty, and my parents, Dave and Shan.

I thank Alex van den Heever and Renias Mhlongo for their friendship and mentorship. Our many hours in the bush together have been a gift I will treasure to the end of my days.

Last, I thank all life trackers the world over. The tracker finds a path where there isn't one, and we need that more than ever.

If you track your authentic life and uncover its meaning, it will catalyze other possibilities for living, and what's important to you will immediately change.

PROLOGUE

I wake at 3 a.m. from that strange midway zone that comes with jet lag.

Outside the open sliding door of my bungalow, the night is silver with moonlight.

Cool winter air seeps in through the mesh of the screen. A scops owl calls every ten seconds—*prrr prrrr prrr*—into the stillness.

I am home. Home in a physical sense. My body knows this place and these night sounds. After months away in the United States, my childhood in the African bush comes flooding back in sensory memories: the smell of the bushveld at night, the unique tone of moonlight, the eternal feeling that the night is somehow happening inside me as it happens around me.

I hear branches snapping like cap guns as an elephant feeds down in the river. High in the ebony tree next to the cottage, a baboon barks into the night: *raaaaahhhh hoooo raaaaahhooo.*

Then, a beat of deep stillness followed by a lion roaring back.

The sound of the lion's roar is the threshold telling me I have stepped from one world to another. After so many nights abroad filled with artificial light and the hum of appliances, there is no truer sound of being home. The timbre of the call, the way it rolls through the cold night air to find me. Its powerful vibrations shudder the door on its hinges. My heart instinctually skips with excitement.

The renowned writer of the African wilderness Laurens van der Post said of the lion's roar that "it is to silence what the shooting star is to the night sky." It is like waking from a dream and having the sensation of being pulled back into my body, as if my soul were being pulled from its endless seeking back into myself by the beauty and power and violence of that ancient sound.

Lying in my bed now, I know the lion is out there in the night. Somehow, more deeply than I can rationally understand, I know his presence is important to me.

Something primal in a part of my brain that stretches back through time barges past the groggy jet-lagged traveler and becomes perfectly and instantly present. Something wild in me is waking up.

I have spent the past ten years charting a strange path between worlds, between my home in the South African wilderness and the fast pace of modern life in the United States. I worked first as a life coach in personal development seminars, then as an apprentice to an indigenous healer. My work has given me a front-row seat to the catalog of illnesses long associated with modern life. Over the years, in conversation after conversation, the themes were the same: abuse, isolation, anxiety, depression on the one hand, and on the other hand an innate creativity and desire to effect change. I saw a deep longing in people to give of themselves, to belong once more to each other and the natural world. So many people I spoke to were searching for a life that felt more meaningful. As was I.

In fact my seeking had taken me all over the world. I had immersed myself in the art forms of personal transformation: Zen meditation, psychology, somatic bodywork, and martial arts were just a few. And yet still I felt there was something I was meant to do that I had not yet discovered. I could sense it out beyond my rational life plan. I could feel its faint edges whispering. I was looking for something. I had found pieces of my own authentic life in wilderness, coaching, South Africa, and America—but how did it all tie together?

Given the paths I had walked so far, I was obviously drawn by the notion that a change in people could change the world. Yet something about the whole business of life coaching never quite sat well with me. Coming from the South African bushveld, I felt pretty certain life did not need a coach. The unbroken stream of life that animates all things is supremely intelligent, and nothing in the wild needs a coach to help it discover what it truly is. If we had lost our way in the modern world—our sense of value, direction, and belonging—it was because we had lost contact with something more instinctual, more innate. All of this shuddered on its mooring in my own subconscious as the roar cut the night.

Still, I knew deeply that I—that we—needed a different direction.

Yet there are no processes in modern society through which to transform. We are a world desperate for change and yet saddled with an outdated momentum. Deep down we all know something else is possible, but how to get there? I came to learn that this transformation could begin in the lives of individuals. No. It *had* to begin in the lives of individuals. Could there be a deeper call to adventure to life, to the edge of what we fear and long for?

Another roar. This land is the keeper of my family's stories. Londolozi Game Reserve, the name derived from the Zulu for "protector of all living things." The presence of lions in my life is like an echo that always rings through to the core of my heart. The farther from home I go, the louder it calls.

My ancestors first came to this wild part of eastern South Africa known as the Lowveld in 1926 to hunt lions. My great-grandfather bought the property when it was still a bankrupt cattle farm. Part of the reason it was bankrupt was because the lions had been eating the cattle. This had been part of its allure.

For three generations, hunting lions was what Vartys did on this piece of land where I now lay, before my parents and uncle transitioned it into a game reserve and safari operation. We no longer hunt lions, but still we pursue them to observe their magnificence. Lions are a part of our mythology. To this day, around campfires, we tell of encounters with these most powerful creatures, encounters that had shown my father and grandfather what it means to be alive. I had been raised on stories of Big Black, a lion whose mane, as black as anthracite, hung down between his legs and whose nature had commanded terror and respect from everyone who encountered him. My history was woven together with theirs.

Londolozi is contiguous with Kruger National Park in

No one can tell you
what your track will be
or how to know what
calls you and brings you to life.
That's your work to do. But a great
tracker can ask: How do
you know you love
something?

the wild eastern part of South Africa, making it part of one of the largest game reserves in the world. Over the years we have seen nomadic lions maraud onto the territory between nightfall and dawn and take control of it. As safari guides, when we venture out each morning, we never know what we might find.

We have come to know many of the lions, but there are still others of unknown temperament that we could meet on any given day. Lions that have charged the open Land Rovers and scared safari guides so profoundly that they instantly resigned. Lions that have caused people to end their safaris early, so they could go home and sit in the safe confines of their manicured gardens.

I see the lion in my mind's eye. It is a creature of astounding athletic proportions. A large male lion can tip the scale at 400 pounds. It can cover the 100-meter dash in four seconds. It regularly takes on prey, such as buffalo, that are double its size. The lion's teeth and claws form an apparatus superbly designed to kill. Most large cats—tigers, leopards, jaguars—are solitary and inclined to avoid fighting, since even a small injury can be fatal. Lions are different, with a mane to defend their head and neck. It is suggested that they have evolved to be inclined toward conflict.

In the bushveld everything speaks. The ground mur-

murs with the footprints of animals that have left their mark. The birds, winged spies. The baboons, sentinels on watch for danger. The lion may have sat up in the grass to roar, which is why the baboon saw him and gave the alarm.

Outside my door, a story is being told in the night. The tracker inside me is waking up to listen. The tracker inside me wants to be part of telling that story.

To track is to discover that nature is alive and speaks a language all its own. To track is to travel the trail of an animal and weave yourself into the tapestry of its story. It is an art that lives inside us, a way of being in union with the natural world.

I have long suspected that we are a culture of forgotten trackers. As a boy, when I was first introduced to tracking, I didn't realize its importance. I took what was in front of me for granted and didn't pay much attention. It was only in my teenage years that the bug started to bite. Even then, I couldn't see that tracking could become a way of life.

I know, as someone who has lived between worlds, how we have lost our connection to nature, to aliveness, to passion and freedom and joy. Modern men and women have fallen into the numbing lure of screens and social networks and poisoned food and jobs that are meaningless. We have forgotten that life holds a unique story for us all. A thread made up of faint signs that lead to the manifestation of something unique. What the native people call "your medicine way." Something that only you can give to the world.

Inside you is the wild part of you that knows what your gift, purpose, and mission are. That part of you is wild and elusive. It cannot be captured, as it is always evolving. To live on its trail, you must become a tracker. In some ways, this book is a mythology. It is the story of the day I found my track. It is my story, but I hope it will be the beginning of a new story for you, and for all of us who want to make a new world.

The roar again. Calling to something deep inside me.

I

THE CALL

I get out of bed at 4 a.m. I move through my room with an old automation. There was a time in my life as a safari guide when this was how every day started. In the hour before the dawn, when the moon is low in the western sky and the world feels like a place of gentle secrets.

I splash water on my face and notice the gray in the stubble and the thinning hair on the top of my head. I am getting older. I consider how my early life as a safari guide had been a strange initiation into a different type of guiding. I am a kind of flawed mirror, by no means wise or actualized, but willing to be in the endless discomfort of asking "Is this life?" As a coach, I'm always challenging that question.

Putting on the clothes in my closet is like putting on an old version of myself. Faded khaki pants, a thick worn

Teesav ranger shirt, the Veldskoens with different-colored laces that I have worn all over the African continent. The person who used to wear these clothes seems long gone, and yet he is standing in this room. I reach for my old tracking stick with a clubbed top, my knife, and my old leather hat. Anyone who goes regularly into the bush has a routine to their departure made of the things they carry with them into the unknown.

Outside, the darkness is lit by kerosene lanterns, and in the clear cold morning air they flicker with an old familiarity. I drive in darkness from my house to Alex's, through the small village of Londolozi. Alex is one of the best trackers in southern Africa, ten years older than me, close enough to get into trouble together, old enough to guide me out of it. A true friend and mentor.

The thatched cottages are still and silent. It is before even the safari guides have begun to stir and prepare for their day.

Alex's house is on the outskirts of the village, which seems appropriate. He lives on the fringe where civilization gives way to wilderness. His house is positioned at the limits of his tolerance for the domestic.

Alex is a paradox. He grew up first in wealth and then in poverty. He was fourteen when his family lost everything, and he told me he could recall a time when he had been so hungry he had waited for a chicken to lay an egg so he could eat. At other times, he hunted rabbits on the lawn of the local inn across from his home, much to the dismay of the local innkeeper. He lived between that reality and the reality of one of the country's top boarding schools paid for by friends and family. There was inside him both a well-educated boy and a poacher. It was this paradox of his psychology that made him a successful tracker.

Alex lived by his wits. He had known an empty belly and was opposed to any authority that was not his own. He had arrived in the bush as a green nineteen-year-old from the coast with a single knowledge inside himself: that this was where he belonged.

His entry into the safari industry had been born of single-minded tenacity. After failing the ranger training course, he refused to leave the lodge. He took a job painting an ablution block and doing other camp chores for months before he was allowed back into the training for another go. He has been here ever since.

When the door opens, Alex appears dressed for a winter's morning. He is short and stocky with a crooked smile and large expressive blue eyes. He wears a woolen hat on his head pulled up like a cone and slightly off to one side. He gives off an air of pending mischief.

The art
of the way
the tracker sees
is the way he can
look at the thing
he has seen
a thousand times
and always see
something new.

Although Alex is white, the position of his hat is characteristically Shangaan. The Shangaan are a Bantu tribe of hunter-gatherers and traders who have lived for generations in the wild territories between South Africa, Mozambique, and southern Zimbabwe. With their curious sense of humor and flair, the Shangaan people have a seemingly endless gift for wearing hats with comic originality. The hat is the jump-off point for a full Shangaan greeting.

"Uri yini mgedeze?" he asks. *What do you have to say, untouchable one?*

"Avuxeni majombaan," I say. *Good morning, small boots.*

"U vuyile I khale ndzi nga ku voni." *You have come back. Long time I haven't seen you.*

Alex is a superb linguist, and his understanding of the Shangaan language has allowed the thought patterns and outlook of the Shangaan people deep into his being. I have seen the joy and surprise on the faces of shopkeepers and old men sitting under trees as they heard their language beautifully spoken by a white man. For Alex, the great-great-grandson of an Afrikaner who was one of the founders of the Afrikaans language, in a country torn apart by racism, his respect for the language and culture of the Shangaan has been an act of embodied healing.

The nicknames are typical of the Shangaan, who have a unique gift for bestowing a name that captures your character. Something about *ma-jom-baan*, small boots, is perfect for Alex, with his diminutive stature and adventurous spirit. For me, he captures the ungrounded nature of my being *mgedeze*, which, with no direct translation, equates to something like "hard to pin down." Some here have always considered me a free spirit, and at times in my life I have lived in the shadow of that name, ill-disciplined and vaguely defined.

The Shangaan are known for being the best trackers in southern Africa. They are a tribe of poets and rogues who abandoned the warring ways of the Zulu to go their own way. Averse to conflict because of their innate open nature, they are a tribe of storytelling observers. They embody the art form of tracking perfectly. They watch, they notice details, they can fall into a story and let it take them on a journey of twists and turns. As mimics they can take on any character and understand a creature from the inside out.

Alex is making coffee, and it feels good to be back in his home, resuming our old ways. These mornings have evolved over the years. Some things are the same: the smell of thatch in his house, the old couch. But other things have changed. There was a time when I would find Alex passed out on the couch in his underpants after a party. But now he is married, and the presence of his wife and daughter still sleeping in the other room brings a more mature feeling to the house, as well as a much nicer aesthetic. Our lives may have changed, but our enthusiasm for going into the bush has not.

"I heard a lion call at about 3 a.m.," I say. "Did you hear it?"

"No, but a hyena called at midnight right outside my window. Woke Bella up. Shit, it was loud." Then suddenly serious, "No one has seen lions for days. The rangers say the guests have been complaining."

We work as a tracking team for the lodge along with Renias. Unhindered by guests, we are able to follow a lion's track for hours in a way that safari guides can't. Once we find them, we tell the guides where to go.

"Ahi fambi hi landza tinghala! *Let's go and track lions!*" Alex says with conviction.

We take our coffee and sit outside by the embers of last night's fire. A nightjar calls somewhere close by. *Dear lord deliver us, dear lord deliver us.*

Then, out of the dark walks Renias Mathanjane Mhlongo.

He arrives in true Renias style, in a state of pure joy. He wears a thick green coat and conical woolen hat.

"Hello guys," he says in a deep voice.

"I don't know where we are going but I know exactly how to get there" might be the motto of the great tracker.

"Avuxeni mathanjane," we reply. *Good morning*.

"Hello buti uvuyile, ndzi tsakile ku ku vona. *I am happy to see you.*" He shakes my hand and holds it for a long time in a way typical of the Shangaan.

Renias is to the bushveld what Laird Hamilton is to the surf of Hawaii. He has a skill and know-how that is beyond anything that can be taught, an innate sense for how the environment works, laid down in the fertile learning grounds of childhood. A true naturalist and wilderness genius, he grew up not far from here hunting and gathering in tune with the old ways. He is a living bridge between the ancient and the modern, embodying a way of living that is being forgotten, even by his own people.

Ren knows how to move through the wilderness with an awareness tuned to every scuff of earth and each sound. He knows how to see what is there, and also what is not there. To hear not just the alarm calls, but the silences. Ren notices uniquely.

When he was a boy his teachers had been hunger and survival. He had learned the natural wisdom that comes of thirst. Renias knows the way of the honeyguide, a bird that leads people to beehives and in return is left a share of the spoils. It's hard to think of something more anciently enchanting and connected than having a wild bird as a guide. Unlike modern men who have been taught to live in competition, Renias lives in profound relation with his surroundings. He knows how to hunt warthogs when they burrow in termite mounds and how to cook a tortoise. In some ways Ren is more in touch with his wild animal nature than anyone I know, and this makes him more truly human.

In the bush, Ren is pure gold. He is the tracker who is called upon when the other trackers lose the trail. He makes things happen around him; little occurrences. He can speak squirrel and can find an owl or a python with his understanding of bird calls. In his presence the word "mastery" comes to mind. To me a master is anyone who can be themselves in any situation. Renias lives this definition. He has achieved one of the hardest things to achieve in our time: a freedom from judgment about how and who he should be.

"Buti, please, you can't give my number as a reference," Alex says to Ren. "I had Ellerines Appliance Store call me ten times yesterday! They say you missed a payment on a CD player."

"That CD player it's not working," says Ren as if he is not to blame.

"And last week I had some workshop in Hazy View

call about new tires on your Toyota." Alex pantomimes a phone next to his ear.

Ren shrugs. He often buys things he doesn't need and he drives Alex crazy, running up debts at appliance stores and taking credit schemes that leave him overpaying for random objects. Alex is the one left fielding calls from debt collectors. Ren doesn't seem to be overly worried about any of this. His unique skills can always earn him money in the bushveld. He doesn't understand the mind-set of saving. Save for what? Life is immediate. There is no future. If you have money, you spend. If you have food, you eat.

It seems like very few things actually worry him. The force of his lightheartedness makes for an intense aura, and I have, on more than one occasion, considered the idea that Renias is perhaps enlightened. Maybe through hours of the intense presence required from tracking, he has experienced a shift in mental consciousness that in the East would come from meditation, but here in Africa comes from the oneness of the trail. Growing up living off the land as a hunter-gatherer has placed in him an immediacy with life that makes him incredibly present and wonderful to be around, yet gives him a terrible debt record.

The three of us sit in the darkness and drink our coffee.

The stars overhead slowly fade as the night spins away on the turn of the earth. I can smell the faint aroma of wood smoke and coffee and feel the cold air on my face. Acacia thorns, long and white, arch over the firepit. Somewhere across the river a giant eagle-owl gives a guttural call.

This is what we do. We wait for lions to roar. It is what we have always done. We are waiting for the call. Ready, awake long before anyone else, listening.

In America, many men in the groups I have facilitated have told me that they feel like they are sleepwalking through their lives. Going through the same routines, falling asleep into social media or the news. They are experiencing a kind of disengagement that makes them feel older than they are. I suspect that part of being a man is that you will as a matter of course fall asleep in your own life. It will happen. Knowing this seems important to me.

The journey out of that will begin not with the call but with the desire to hear the call. The desire itself has an energy. Part of waking yourself, it seems to me, is made by paying attention. Most of us are looking but not seeing. The same men who had told me about falling asleep in their lives reported amazing things when they turned their attention back on and started to tune in and listen for a path back to life. The ancients call this essential knowledge.

As trackers our part is to be awake. Our part is to listen. We want to hear the call.

Tracking begins with wanting to track.

Out from across the last shadows of night it comes. A booming sound wave through the thick cold air. *Roaaaar rooooaaaaah.*

We turn our heads toward the sound.

Ren cups his ears to enhance it. I can see him throwing a mental stone out over the woodlands and clearings of vast wilderness, trying to land it close to that lion. Volume, direction, local knowledge of the game paths, tenor: All of it forms an equation. A place to begin.

In the quiet of the morning, the lion's roar stands out. To one who has fallen asleep in life, it switches on the attention.

The roar brings a shift in Renias's energy. The bush exerts a kind of pull on him, as if he were one pole of a magnet and the call the other. He wants to go look for that lion. No, it's deeper than that. He has to go.

—

"Sounds like a male somewhere near Lex's Pan," Renias says of the water hole named after a renowned game ranger. "In that area I think. Ahi fambi." *Let's go.*

The light is now pale, and the trunks of the marula trees are a faded blue.

We can't be sure where the lion roared; the wilderness is vast, and the chance of finding a track and following it presents a challenge of immense difficulty, even before adding in the fact that lions bite. But the tracker's instinct is always to go into the unknown. We live with an intense curiosity. It is the means by which life pulls us to a destiny bigger than what we could have imagined for ourselves. We thrive on it and know that every time we go, we invite a process that will put us into an encounter with life.

For Renias and Alex, the unknown is a discipline of wildness, and wildness is a relationship with aliveness. Too much uncertainty is chaos, but too little is death.

2

TRACK AWARENESS

We head out to an old Land Rover with its roof sawn off and seats placed in rising tiers upon its back. This Landy is one that has worked hard mileage in the safari game, and now, with an undercarriage long past its prime, a battered steering wheel, and the four-wheel-drive knob missing, it has been given to us to use as a tracking vehicle.

There is a brief ritualized argument about who will drive. Driving on a cold morning is not fun, and hands have been known to become clawlike on the wheel in the open air.

"Mgedeze. Get behind the wheel there," says Alex.

While spoken casually, it's a clear directive from my mentor. In the tracking rankings, which are effectively the chain of command, it is clear: Renias, Alex, and then me. Not that they would ever state this rank or hierarchy.

Nature doesn't see status or wealth or social position. It cares only about presence, one's ability to read the signs, navigate the terrain, and translate the language of the wilderness. Nature is the great equalizer.

In the bush this kind of order is not prescribed; it is born out of the honesty of the natural world. Nature doesn't see status or wealth or social position. It cares only about presence, one's ability to read the signs, navigate the terrain, and translate the language of the wilderness. Nature is the great equalizer.

Alex learned this lesson early on in his career. He was twenty years old and had just begun working as a safari guide at Londolozi. Renias was his tracker. They worked together as a team, showing safari-goers the big five: lion, leopard, rhino, buffalo, and elephant. Alex, green and full of the arrogance of youth, was under the impression that he was competent and clued in. He knew the lay of the land. He had an education and interacted easily with the guests. He knew the botanical names of all the trees. Renias, by contrast, couldn't read or write. He had never been to school. Surely he shouldn't have the upper hand? It took a female leopard all of fifteen minutes to set the record straight.

The Tugwaan female, named after a dense riverbed where she made her territory, was a leopard that was known for being unpredictable. She was small and wiry with frayed ears. I once heard her described as "steel cables wrapped in velvet." She made her territory in a thickly shaded dry riverbed that seemed to reflect her secretive nature.

Driving down the road, Renias saw her tracks in the soft sand of the drainage line where the road cut through it.

"Ingwe," he said. *Leopard.*

No wild animal has
ever participated
in a should.

Alex stopped the vehicle and the two men got out to look at the tracks and try to gauge their freshness. It looked like the leopard had passed that way in the last few hours, and they decided to follow her.

Alex, full of bravado, turned to the guests. "You all please stay here in the Land Rover. Renias and I are going to walk down to the river to follow these tracks." With a swagger he removed his rifle from its rack on the hood. "When I return, we will have found you a leopard. Sit tight."

Now Alex carried the rifle so he was, in theory, in charge of his and Renias's safety. Ren followed the tracks as they led deeper down into the shade of the riverbed. What happened next is the stuff of bushveld nightmares. Alex and Renias walked straight into the Tugwaan female's den, where she had a small cub.

Moments like this have a strange disorientation to them: a few minutes ago you were driving the Land Rover in your dream job and chatting to some tourists, the next you are over the lip of the abyss of death. The speed of the change is almost impossible to grasp.

The leopard burst out of the shadows, a blur of fangs and rage. Her growl was like a dirt bike at full revs. She flew up the drainage line in a zigzagging blur. Leopards are feared the world over for their speed and for the damage they can inflict when they explode upward, attacking the head and neck with their jaws and forepaws and raking the body with their back legs.

As the space between the leopard and Alex closed in a blink, he took a step back in fright and fell over a log. The rifle flew from his hands. He lay sprawled on his back, and as he sat up the leopard slammed on the brakes, stopping her charge almost at his feet. She stood over him, snarling with a deathly menace.

Alex told me later that he was certain she was going to kill him. He had sand in his mouth from where she had braked in the soft gravel. Adrenaline caused his visual acuity to become so sharp that he could see with superb clarity her gums vibrating.

Right at that moment, he heard the quiet, steady voice of Renias behind him. "Majombaan unga ndzi languti matihlo. *Alex, don't look her in the eye.* Majombaan yima, yima. *Small boots, wait, wait.*"

Renias was using his own steady energy to shape the outcome of the moment. He was using his own calm to keep Alex calm and to calm the leopard and show her their intention. To move fast and rush could have been misinterpreted as aggression, so in the tradition of the natural world and with his life as his guide, Renias spoke in the ancient language of the animal's energy. He used his body language, his movement, and the tone of his voice to create and convey a feeling, not just to Alex, but to the leopard. In a situation in which things were happening incredibly fast, by being slow, Renias was able to create time.

He watched her with the eye of the tracker, an eye trained to notice the subtleties of the leopard's energy and body language. When they shifted, it was almost imperceptible, accompanied only by a tiny change in the tenor of her growl. It was then that Renias said to Alex, "Now, move back slowly."

This is the movement that could have caused the leopard to pounce. But Ren called the exit perfectly. Alex moved backward and the leopard held her ground. Alex felt Renias's hand on his shoulder, perfectly calm, as he slowly led him to safety.

That's how mentors should be made: not through titles or words but through actions. On the ground, in the face of a leopard, one feels acutely alone. To be guided in a moment like that, with such extreme stakes, creates a bond that is rare in modern life.

From then on, Alex dedicated himself to learning the ancient art of tracking. His arrogance had been vaporized. In its place, Alex recognized a man who could teach him what he truly wanted to learn. For the next ten years, Renias and Alex ran safaris together and Renias taught Alex how to speak Shangaan and the ways of the bush.

What Alex was most struck by was that Renias never shamed or belittled him about falling over and dropping his rifle. The bush had been the teacher and there was nothing more to say.

Behind the wheel of the Landy, the engine sputters and chokes as I fire the ignition. A little puff of smoke in the clear air and we are off. Alex sits next to me and Renias sits up on a seat welded to the hood called the tracker seat. Cats often travel along game paths, and this spot allows Renias to see the tracks on the road as the dawn breaks.

With his coat and blanket wrapped against the morning cold, Renias looks like a mountain of a man, and he is. In his mid-fifties, muscular and strong, with thick forearms, wide shoulders, and a naughty smile, he is the embodiment of a likeable rogue. As if on cue, he turns in his seat and announces to us, "Buti, you know I have never been turned down by a woman. It is because I ate a lot of warthog meat as a child, gives my body a good smell." He laughs intensely at his own joke. Ren often unleashes unsolicited fun facts.

As we drive out of the camp it's still dark. The lights

of the houses are beginning to blink on one by one. The other guides are just starting to stir and gather their provisions for their morning safaris. Shapes of men carrying rifles move like shadows in the predawn. A hyena walks through the camp looking guilty.

Five minutes out, the eastern sky ripens into a deep orange and the sun peeks over the horizon. Animals tend to move during these cool hours just after sunrise. The low light creates contrast on the ground, causing tracks to pop. The magnetism of these early hours is palpable. Later, the morning will warm, the cats will move to the shade, and the dawn energy will give way to a lazy heat. The witching hour in Africa is the middle of the day, still and hot and unmoving. The middle of the day is more a time for ghosts than midnight is.

We have only a few golden hours for tracking, and I can feel all of us eager to get on the trail. The dirt road we are on has not been driven since yesterday afternoon, so to Renias, sitting on the front, it is full of the information of animal movement: the tracks of a male leopard, a porcupine that trundled along dropping the odd quill, the fresh tracks of two male nyala antelope. Moments after seeing the tracks, we see the nyala beside us stalking around each other in a slow-motion dressage-like display to establish dominance. Ancient people would have watched their animal kin move, and those early imitations became the first dances. It's easy to see the foundations of human culture when one is in the wild.

Watching Renias marking all of this from the front of the Land Rover, it's easy for me to follow the trail of his ancestors back to the roots of science, back to the roots of art, when an ancient tracker saw a print in soft sand and realized that the abstract shape represented something. His first premises and deductions laid out in earth and interpreted as a means of survival.

Tracking shaped our evolving intelligence. Tracking was the first story our species ever told. And when you follow an animal's trail you are linked to every person who has ever read the earth, every ancient culture that has walked a trail. Tracking is a birthright for every person, a memory of how to converse with nature.

We pass a herd of elephants feeding on the combretum veld. "They like to feed now. Do you know why?" Ren turns to ask me.

Before I can answer, he continues, "I think it's because the branches have dew on them and so they like how juicy it is. That's what I think."

It's a question I have never even thought to ask, and it contains an insight into a weakness of mine: I tend to just accept what I see. Ren always looks closer, he always asks why. He has a gift for examining the wallpaper of life.

The art of the way the tracker sees is the way he can look at the thing he has seen a thousand times and always see something new. Renias has been out in the bush every morning of his life. He is fifty-five years old. And each day he looks at it anew and asks "Why?"

Two hippos cross our path on their way to a water hole. I breathe in and try to see them through new eyes. The bushveld is a landscape that holds feelings. There is an unseen presence, a feeling akin to the reverence conjured inside a beautiful cathedral.

Obsessed with perfection and doing it right, we want to go straight to the "lion." We don't realize the significance of the path of first Tracks and how to be invested in a Discovery rather than an Outcome.

Unseen, but felt. The intangible presence people long for. Wilderness is a space of relation, a place where the separation of language gives way to union.

I remember a time once in a forgotten part of the Zambezi Valley where I spent a week looking for one of the world's rarest birds, the Pel's fishing owl. I walked the riverbank each day looking up into shaded mahogany trees and trying to find its daytime perch. I found feathers and a horizontal branch that arched out over a still pool. Fish scales told me this was where the owl made its nighttime fishing spot. I was tracking a creature that never touched the ground. Yet to the tracker there were signs.

At night I lay awake in my tent, alone for miles in every direction, and heard the strange ghostlike call as the owl taunted me from the darkness.

The Pel's fishing owl is a bird whose presence manifests itself only in the deepest wilderness. Light, loud sounds, or any of the things that come with the ways of people are against the owl's nature. The owl is a symbol that you are in a wild place where few people will ever venture; where the environment conveys a nature deep within your own being. There's a low-lying depression and anxiety plaguing modern life—a symptom of an undiagnosed homesickness to feel a belonging to the greater ecosystem and know ourselves in relation rather than isolation.

When I did find the bird in the late evening on the seventh day of my quest, it looked down at me with the blackest eyes I have ever seen. Eyes that seemed to penetrate into me with their darkness. In that moment, I knew something very important was happening. I am a person who likes secrets, and I am a person who has felt that I can only truly know myself in forgotten places. I was meeting something long forgotten by our world, something in the track of wilderness. A stillness that at one time would have been the most natural state of our collective being. It is in these encounters that wilderness brings us closer to places in ourselves that often go unvisited in modern life.

This is what I am always seeking. This is what I am trying to help others find.

The Landy bumps down the road past old leadwood and flowering knobthorn trees. Alex sits quietly beside me in the easy silence of old friendship. We cross a small drainage line called the *masavene*, the river of sand. Renias holds up his hand.

"Famba ka tsongo. *Go slow,*" he says.

After about twenty minutes of driving we are approaching Lex's Pan, the area where Renias thinks the lion's roar might have come from. Out of the drainage line, the land widens to an open dusty area with the water hole on its northern end. The ground has been churned into a fine white powder by animals coming to drink. The pan is a muddy hollow in the ground.

"Yima kwalani. *Stop in this place*," says Ren as he hops off the tracker seat.

"Let's look," says Alex.

We walk slowly across the ground. There are a myriad of tracks on the earth. Information laid down in layers, a sequence of events held by the earth. When I walk across it I see a simple two-dimensional drawing: the zebra tracks on top of the wildebeest, then some warthogs over them, all coming to drink.

For Renias, and perhaps for Alex too, I imagine this same scene is like walking through a three-dimensional hologram. Images of animals appear in an almost live order of appearance as the information before us is processed with incredible detail. A three-dimensional narrative of what transpired around the water hole plays in their mind's eye. The track tells much more than just which animals were there. Small cameos of behavior are there to be interpreted: the gouged earth where a duiker bolted, the long regal steps of a slow-moving giraffe. Each track holds a mood, movement, and cadence.

When I was a boy, Renias would take me to a game path, the open trail created by the animals as they traveled from clearing to water.

"Walk down it and tell me what you see," he would instruct.

I would walk down the trail and see the tracks of a herd of impala and then the massive four-toed foot of a hippo.

"Hippo and impala," I would report.

"Famba uya languta futhi." *Go look again*.

The next time, I would notice under the hippo track a washed-out genet track, where a squirrel had bounded toward a tree, and where a hornbill had dust-bathed.

"Now walk and listen," Renias would say. Then, "Walk, listen, and smell."

Each time, there would be more information. It was like I was an instrument tuning myself to the information around me. Later in my life, I would come to realize that becoming aware of such information and the feelings it evokes — the people who are important to you, the things that bring you to life, the arrival of something meaningful — is its own kind of consciousness: track awareness. You can easily miss this information if you don't know how to see. Track awareness is how attuned you are to what is around you. It is recognizing a track when it appears. It is teaching yourself how to see what is important to you.

I remember another day as a teenager when the obsession for tracking was truly beginning to take me. We were tracking a lion through thick inhospitable terrain and a baked substrate. Ren was in a hurry to get home, so he figured it would be good to get the job done fast. He moved like a bullet on the trail. I remember breaking into a run at times to keep up with him. He circled tracks with his stick as we went, but even then, they remained invisible to me.

"You must train yourself to see your track," he said.

In the hour and a half it took us to find the lion, I couldn't make out one clear track. Where else in my life was there a path that I was missing? The implications felt profound.

I was struck by this as a tracker, but later when I began to coach and work with people in ceremony, it took on an entirely new depth. The idea that life is full of information. "You must train yourself to see what you are looking for."

Part of why this isn't as simple as it sounds is that it's not rational. You can't think your way to a calling. Finding what is uniquely yours requires more than rationality. You have to learn how your body speaks. You have to learn how you know what you know. You have to follow the inner tracks of your feelings, sensations, and instincts, the integrity and truth that are deeper than ideas about what you should do. You have to learn to follow a deeper, wiser, wilder place inside yourself.

Track awareness is the ability to read the field of life with discernment and yet also know your inner landscape. Everything in the natural world knows how to be itself. Trees know how to greet the spring with buds, and bees are drawn naturally to flowers. Leopards from birth know they are keepers of solitude, while lions are made for the pride. We are a part of nature, and inside each of us is a wild self that knows deeply what it is meant to do. Inside each of us is a natural innate knowledge of why we are here. Tracking is a function of directing attention, bringing our awareness back to this subtle inner trail of the wild self, and learning to see its path.

Yet most of us have so much of the social conditioning of modern life that the track of the wild self has been lost. We live with our attention directed outward. We focus on the social cues of our culture. We look to others to define our path and value and purpose. We lose ourselves in shoulds.

Shoulds are full of traps — traps laid by society and your limited rules for yourself. No wild animal has ever participated in a should. What you know to do is deeper than that. No one can tell you what your track will be or how to know what calls you and brings you to life. That's your work to do. But a great tracker can ask: How do you know you love something? How do you feel when you are fully expressing yourself? Learn that feeling and then start looking, not for the thing, but for the feeling. It's there if you can tune yourself to it, if you can learn to see how the field of life is always speaking to you. Attention shapes the direction of the tracker's life. We must turn our attention back to the wild self.

Renias does that now in the dust. He moves in ever-widening arcs, scanning the ground churned by the feet and hooves of hundreds of creatures. He is relaxed. There is no concern that he will miss it. He is not even concerned with finding it. He is completely open to the landscape around him.

Before he even becomes conscious that he has seen it, he reacts. Like a boxer whose body has a memory faster than conscious thought. Amidst the myriad of scuffmarks and hoofmarks, amidst dung and wood, amidst a million pixels of information, through all the noise in a wilderness the size of a small European country, he picks the track of the lion. He has put himself in range of the call, and now, almost magically, he has woven the thread of our lives across the faint thread of the lion's trail.

He has seen what he is looking for. He has trained himself to see it. This is how we cut the track.

3

THE TRACKS OF THE FATHER

Renias, Alex, and I are walking in the land of our fathers.

The father washes onto the son. He lives inside you as an aspiration, a disappointment, or a fear. Afraid you will never be like him or afraid you will be; he is there in the bones of your emotions. In the voices in your head. In your expectations of yourself. In the shadows of your weakness or strength. No matter how good the relationship, there is a tension between father and son.

The father is a track: a trail we choose to follow or a path we walk away from. Renias and Alex have chosen to walk in a different direction than their fathers.

Renias's father was a dangerous man who beat his sons. As a result, Ren had a conditioned awareness born of this danger. They say that the children of alcoholics know what the night will hold by the sound of the keys hitting the hallway table. They develop a sharp perception for signs, sounds, and even the feeling of a room. Sometimes our medicine comes in strange ways. Renias's childhood with his father meant he didn't miss a thing. It gave him what he would need to be a skillful tracker as well as superior social skills. He was able to notice the subtleties of social interaction and quickly put people at ease. In his travels around the globe with Alex, he was able to fit into foreign social interactions by being easily attuned to people and social cues. Ren's quality as a tracker was made of this awareness. His father had taught him to notice and deduct; as a tracker these skills were always with him.

Alex's father had been an introverted, introspective man uninterested in cultural ideals of masculinity. As a young boy Alex had been drawn to the same ideals his father had rejected and as a result developed an aggressive tenacity in response to his mild-mannered dad.

One time out in the bush, Alex and two other rangers were riding bicycles when they came across a herd of elephants that were feeding in the road ahead of them. They stopped their bicycles and stood watching the herd from some distance. Suddenly, the ground started to shudder, and from behind them came a terrible sound, like the crack of automatic gunfire. Alex looked over his shoulder to see the matriarch elephant, which had been separated from the herd, bearing down on them.

The bicycles had allowed the men to approach quickly and silently. Now their position between the cow and her herd caused her to panic, which made her deadly. What sounded like gunfire had been medium-sized trees exploding as she charged like a semi truck toward them.

One of the rangers dropped his bike and ran into the bush. The other threw himself and his bike behind a thick clump of brush. Alex, the legacy of his father inside him, did what was instinctual to him: he jumped back on his bike and rode headlong into the herd. The sort of man who always wanted to step away had made Alex the sort of man who went straight in.

The bike pedals creaked under the force of his acceleration as he felt the enraged and panicked matriarch closing ground on him. He expected at any minute to be ironed.

He closed the distance to the herd in front of him in seconds and swerved past a young bull and between an old cow and a young calf. The cow swung her trunk over his head. He ducked under its hydraulic decapitating power. The entire herd was screaming and grumbling. Alex waited to die. And then suddenly, there was distance between him and the herd. Still pedaling, he looked back over his shoulder and saw the matriarch standing over the other ranger's abandoned bike, murdering it with blunt tusks and using her knees to crush it.

When Alex rolled into camp, his blue eyes were wide with shock. By the time I arrived at his house he was drinking a neat scotch.

"Chap, that elephant nearly ironed me," he said. "That's one of the closest calls I've ever had."

But there it was: the inclination to go into life that had been with him his whole life. The gift of wild tenacity that his father had given him.

Then there was my father. The man who had created this wild place. A visionary in so many ways. I never had any doubts about the beauty of my father's heart, but he had been raised in the old hunting ways of "work it out" that shamed me into learning. "You don't know how to make a fire? Work it out!" "You don't know how to skin a carcass? Work it out!" The words had such shameful scorn. I could hear his father and his father's father's voice barking out of his mouth. A trauma pattern traveling through time.

I had always been expected to work things out. But he overestimated my capability. I often didn't know how to do this, and the scorn made me think I should know, even if I had never been shown. This made for a terrible uncertainty and sense of inadequacy in me. My ability never seemed to match his expectations. This is common between the father and the son, the dynamic making for an innate tension. This is why in native traditions, the mentor to the young man is never the father but a close male relative.

Alex and Renias had been a huge part of the journey of learning to trust myself. Particularly Alex, who, having been mentored by Ren, became a mentor to me. Trauma can travel, but so can healing.

I remember a whole summer in high school when Alex and I lived together in his small house. Mentorship in men is often a kind of transmission born of physical proximity; the teaching is not spoken but absorbed. For thousands of years, men danced and walked and moved together, taught each other the ways of nature. They slept under the stars and rested in the shade of old trees. They told stories and taught each other by being together, facing real danger together.

Men need these dimensions of wilderness and the unknown to know the more primal part of their own psyche and body.

Every morning Alex would take me out to track rhinos, slowly showing me how to fall into the movement of that animal. He taught me how to look for the way its front feet cut down into the grass and the strange half-moon of its toe. Like Renias, Alex would let me lead and then guide me when I lost the track, but the feeling was always of tracking together. It was a subtle sharing that felt supportive but not condescending.

When men track, they are in resonance with every tracker who ever lived. They are in an ancient union with that lineage that helps them know who they are even as their own father as a god or tyrant loses his importance to the greater collective connection. The energy that was moving between Ren, Alex, and myself was a re-fathering. In its purest form, the archetype of the father guides you to be your best. We were finding a way through mentorship to give this to each other.

It was a deep time for me. I felt myself learning. I felt the gratitude of being taught. When someone shares with you, you become someone who wants to share. The competence I felt growing in me was a kind of remedy to the shame I had felt.

In the afternoons we would run through the intense African heat and lift weights in the rudimentary gym at the edge of camp. I got stronger and fitter, and I began to think of myself as a tracker. Some nights we would drink. Other nights we would go and walk in the moonlight, thrilled by the wild aliveness of danger and the alertness it awakened.

After weeks of going out together, my understanding of tracking started to change.

Tracking is very much like learning a foreign language. Single tracks are words. You might see a few as you walk the trail, and they create a jerky first phrase. If you stop speaking and don't practice, the learning recedes, while the more you do it the more natural and fluid it becomes.

One afternoon the short phrases became flowing sentences. I was out alone as Alex had some work to do back at the camp. I came across the tracks of a large rhino bull that had wallowed in a water hole, his body caked in the thick black mud. The track away from the water hole was fairly easy to follow because as the rhino walked through the thick bush, a slick of mud had scrapped off on the trees and bushes. His body was dripping with a Hansel and Gretel trail that I could easily follow from bush to muddied bush.

After a few miles of tracking this, I knew the mud on his body had begun to dry, and the dripping trail became more and more faint, and then there was no more mud. My eyes seamlessly shifted from the mud to the three-toed clover tracks he had left, and suddenly all the iterations of the track that my brain had stored as search images began to pop. I saw the track with ease; I noticed compressions, scuffmarks, smoothed bark where his 3-tonne body had brushed against a tree. I saw the grass laid flat and the imprint of a side toe. The half-moon of a front toe! I was moving on his track, fast and fluent. The easy trail had helped me get out of my own head so that I could relax into myself.

It was easy and natural and I had the feeling that I had gained entry into an entirely new dimension. I could anticipate the subtle shifts of his path, picking up the faintest of tracks like they were elaborate signs. In the same way that after months of being an outsider on a French exchange, the language comes and you suddenly belong to France, to the place, to the culture, the people. Suddenly, I was part of the story of the bush.

The trail was long and the whole time I was on it there was no thought of "me." The "me" shifted into something much larger than myself. I was completely engaged and forgot about time and all of my own little neuroses. As I disappeared, I felt the flow of the animals and the trees, the birds and the silent presence of the clouds. In this unity everything became innately meaningful. Even my own presence in that moment was free from the past and the future. It was more than enough for me to simply be in the experience. I realized the whole purpose of my life was manifest not as some distant outcome but here, inside an infinite state of enoughness.

Before that day, I had always thought that I needed to be somebody in the world. That rhino and the path he walked told me something different: don't try to be someone, rather find the thing that is so engaging that it makes you forget yourself.

In a woodland clearing just before sunset, I found the bull. The wind was in my favor, and coupled with his poor eyesight, I was able to get within a few yards of him. All day he had laid a trail with his prehistoric feet for me to follow. Now, alone with him, I felt inside myself a deep sense that he had guided me to the state of eternal consciousness in which all wild creatures dwell. A wordless land where no thought moves to separate us, and self-consciousness is replaced by seamless unity.

In that state came a deep gratitude for Alex's teachings that stretched through him to Renias. Even though they were not there with me, their presence lived inside me in what had been shared.

I had learned how to learn. In a way the ancient people understood, the mentor unlocked the pressure between father and son. With this new confidence I could finally expect myself to "work it out" with a deeper confidence, and there I found my father's willingness to go bravely at any task with a new courage.

The track of the father is to find him within you. To find what he gave you and what he didn't give you. You must use both sides. The medicine of transformation is innately built into this relationship.

4

THE FIRST TRACK

Renias gives a short whistle to catch our attention. He curls his hand into a fist with his index finger pointed downward in the signal for "on the tracks." We have developed a series of whistles and hand signals among us over the years to find each other in thick bush. A sharp shriek says "back on the tracks." A long disappointed toot indicates no tracks.

Renias begins to move on the trail, and I watch as he lets the lion into his body. He begins to adopt the cadence of the track, and he picks up speed as he walks to match the lion's steps. For Renias this is almost intuitive. He allows the intelligence of his body to mirror the movement of the lion, and in this way he enters a kind of resonance with the animal.

The American tracker Tom Brown says, "The first track is one end of a string. On the other end, a creature is moving." The line that runs from the first track to the creature prowling somewhere out ahead is kinetic. It conveys the animal's mood, the cadence of gait, the speed and behavior. Is he marking territory by leaving telltale scraping marks? Is he loping on a lazy walk to water? Is he moving quickly in hopes of finding another male that has entered his territory to challenge him to a fight? To the tracker, the trail of his track is full of this dynamic information.

Renias knows the instrument of the body as wild and natural and full of instinctual wisdom. He knows to think but also to feel. He uses the way his body feels moving on the track to feel the lion. As I watch Renias now I am struck by how disconnected we are from the body. Obsessed with thinking, modern culture has forgotten the innate knowledge of the body. How its signals are a guide, how it knows what it needs to be healthy. How it can tell you if something is right for you or not by the way it feels. We must learn to read the subtle tracks of the body, the way it relaxes and opens when something feels right, the contraction and tightness when we are not where we are meant to be. Sometimes the body will have to get sick before we will listen to what it is saying to us. For men, feelings have long been outlawed. We have been disconnected from our instincts. Bringing attention back to the landscape of the body allows you to find the trail of the wild self.

We must learn to read
the subtle tracks of the body, the way
it relaxes and opens when something
feels right, the contraction and tightness when
we are not where we are Meant to be . . .
Bringing attention back to the
landscape of the body
allows you to find
the trail of the
wild self.

When I get closer to the trail, I see more rationally what Renias has computed mystically. Endless hours spent tracking have reprogrammed him almost subconsciously. His mastery has transcended the step-by-step process and has harmonized and integrated him in the way you might drive a car without thinking about it. He is doing a lot of difficult things while appearing to do nothing.

What took Ren a moment to compute, I take in slowly. The broad back pad tells us the lion's size is that of a full-grown male. Looking closer, I see his track superimposed over the track of a nocturnal scrub hare, telling of the lion's passage at dawn after the hares had gone to ground. The back foot of the lion, which is more conical in shape, is landing a good few inches in front of the more circular indent of the front paw, telling us that he is walking fast. A lion at this speed will walk you off your feet, opening the gap between you and him with every mile. Lions are formidable walkers.

You have a first track. If you go and get some of what you need, you might get a second first track.

"I don't think we will catch up with him," I say.

"Hi ta swi kuma. *We will get,*" says Renias.

He is supremely confident. Rather than criticizing and tearing down, the voice inside him motivates and builds. It is what in the world of coaching we call supportive self-talk. "I don't know where we are going but I know exactly how to get there," he says.

I stop, feeling the importance of this idea move inside me. Ren has dropped phrases like this on me at different junctures in my life. Single sentences in offhand, sometimes broken English that seem to capture so much of the journey I am on. Like a tracking Zen roshi.

I don't know where we are going but I know exactly how to get there might be the motto of the great tracker.

"Track. Track. Track," Ren has said to me at other times. I understood him to mean find the first track, then the next first track, then the one after that. He does not set out into the unlikely chance of finding a lion in the future. He works with what he has now, in the moment. Joseph Campbell said, "If you can see your whole life's path laid out then it's not your life's path." In the bush and in life, we don't get trails fully laid out. We get tremendous unknowns and, if we are lucky, first tracks. Then next first tracks.

In my own life, I have often struggled with the first

track. Full of grand visions and the desire to do something great, I often couldn't find the first small beginning and then the next small beginning. I couldn't dial huge possibilities into small practical actions. I couldn't trust that doing enough of what needed to be done today would, with time, render a path and an outcome that could be great. I had to learn to be in the process of transformation, not trying to be transformed. You can't skip past creating to the creation.

Here it is again in front of me, brought to life in real time. The vision of the lion, the hope of finding it, begins here with a three-tiered lobe surrounded by four neat toes: the imprint of a cat's foot the size of a man's hand.

If you were to zoom out from this first pugmark, you would see three men in a clearing framed by the ancient sculptured shapes of ten dead leadwoods. Zoom out still farther and you would see Londolozi Game Reserve. Pull the focus wider and Londolozi becomes a speck inside the 10 million acres of wilderness that make up the greater Limpopo Transfrontier Park, which unites the world-famous Kruger National Park in South Africa, Limpopo National Park in Mozambique, and Gonarezhou National Park in Zimbabwe. The first park to unite three nations.

This piece of wilderness has a magnetism. It was the place of my childhood and the home of my imagination.

Alex had dreamed of moving to the bushveld for as long as he could remember. One of his first childhood memories was of glimpsing the bush out the window of the family car on a holiday to Kruger National Park. To a boy from the coast, the terrain was intensely dry, the heat almost hostile. It spoke of a need for hardness; a place to make you a man. Renias knew this too, for he was raised by the land only a few miles south.

So many things had to happen for us three to be here on this day, on this trail. Here in the wilderness, our lives were woven together by a strange fate. To find a particular animal within an area this size might incline one to just stay home, and yet to the tracker, with the mentality to dial the impossibly vast down to a first track, everything became possible.

I thought of all the people I had met who wanted a full vision for a new life and then to move from where they were straight into it. I thought of all the people who had told me that when they knew exactly what they wanted to do, they would leave the soul-destroying thing that they were currently involved with. Obsessed with perfection and doing it right, we want to go straight to the "lion." We don't realize the significance of the path of first tracks and how to be invested in a discovery rather than an outcome.

Watching Alex and Renias's elation at the sight of the

first track and then staring beyond them to a wilderness that dwarfed them and an almost impossible sense that we could find a single feline moving in all that terrain, I remembered a man I had met in a workshop I was facilitating in the Utah mountains. In our conversation, he told me he was burned-out with work and family life. He said he wanted to find his way to a more peaceful place inside himself. The workshop was full of talk but he wanted action, he said, he wanted to be transformed. It's common to think that if we can get the external metrics right everything will be okay. But that does not always leave us the room to learn about ourselves.

I asked him to be quiet for a moment. "What do you need?" I asked.

He immediately started into a story. "I don't get to ask that. I have responsibilities, it's not about me!"

"I know that story," I said. "Go deeper. What do you need?"

He sat for a long moment, then, annoyed, looked at me and said, "I need to be alone for a while. I need some time completely alone. But then what?"

"Don't jump to then what," I replied. "You have a first track. If you go and get some of what you need, you might get a second first track."

The journey to transformation is a series of first tracks.

I don't know where I'm going but I know exactly how to get there.

Back on the trail, we have the first track. We go back to the Land Rover and drop our jackets, knowing that walking will warm us up. We grab our hats, and Alex and I put on sunscreen. Ren pulls his long combretum wood tracking stick from underneath the seat. He uses it to circle tracks, to remove branches, and in extreme cases, to ram down a lion's throat, inducing its gag reflex and forcing it to release whatever person it is mauling. The last use indicating that someone is having a pretty lousy morning.

Without saying it, we know that we are now entering into an unspoken agreement to keep each other safe. The bush is not a place of inevitable menace, as it is often portrayed in movies and on the endless shows about deadly creatures on the wildlife networks. The bush simply has its way. If we respect this and pay attention, we belong here as much as any other animal. But the margins for error are small, and the way one behaves in a high-risk situation is critical. Yet for all of us a life with no sharp edges would be worse. The hazard of modern times is the danger of no danger.

The bush is a place where one must speak the language

of presence; in this way it teaches you about yourself. For example, if a lion were to charge, it is critical to meet the charge by standing your ground and showing the lion your own steady strength. To stand your ground means to disrupt the hardwiring in the predator's instinctual makeup. They are used to things running away.

Homo sapiens on the great plains of Africa evolved along with lions. Where there were lions, there was meat. Our ancestors tracked them in order to steal their kills. They went to battle against them in the defense of livestock. Renias is one of the last people on the planet who is a living window into our past. He grew up with the old ways, under the guidance of his uncle Engen Mhlongo, who was a wild man and superb naturalist. Engen could snare animals with old bits of fencing wire and could make a bow and arrow and then cook up a potent poison using the roots of an impala lily to add a deadly poison to the tip.

When Engen couldn't snare them an antelope, one of the primary ways that Ren's family would get the meat they needed in their calorie-negative hunter-gatherer lifestyle was to track lions in the hope of coming across them feasting on a freshly killed animal and then try to steal the lions' meat. This was no casual pastime. Lions on meat are a terrifying sight. They growl with savage menace while acting as sinew- and bone-ingesting machines. Occasionally fights break out as one lion infringes on another's section of intestine or hindquarter.

To disrupt this blood-covered group of serial killers requires profound courage and a hunger in your own belly to make you bold. This is what Renias and his brothers used to do. Charge in and with their bold courage try to scare the lions off long enough to cut a thick piece of their meat to eat. Sometimes the lions ran off in fright, other times they didn't.

Watching Renias move now, I am struck by how differently his time in the bush has shaped his outlook. Renias lives outside the deceptions of modern life. Its structured psychological outlook has not affected him, and I know that he is a living clue to a different way of being. He doesn't concern himself with the attainment of status or wealth. He doesn't worry about his security in the future or his position within a social group. He doesn't talk about politics or worry that he isn't doing enough. To him, time is not money. Productivity is not a reflection of his value. He considers treadmills ridiculous. When it's time to work, he works. When it's time to rest, he rests.

It's hard to grasp the change in the quality of your consciousness until you have spent a few days and then weeks and then months in a wilderness. Seeing someone who simply doesn't have the social programming you do is profound because it forces you to see that a huge part of what you might think of as "this is how I am" or "this is what you do" is not you at all but patterns of behavior and thinking you have adopted from the cultural story. You have been told what to be and want. This realization is immense as it is the beginning of a much deeper question about what we actually want.

You are your outlook, and that outlook is not universal. It was given to you. The aboriginals used to say of modern life, "It's three days deep." In three days in wilderness, you learn what's important and your mind changes. Your way of being shifts.

There is an immediacy to life in the wilderness that makes so much of what most of us consider important fall away. In the bush I notice how my body falls into a wise rhythm set by light and heat and cold. I move in the dawn, rest through the day, and sleep at night. I eat when I'm hungry. I forget what I look like. I'm surprised to find that the world doesn't end, and in fact I become happier and less lonely with each day. I transition from endless doing into a steady being. Occasionally, some task that I need to do will arise crisply out of nowhere. I notice it, attend to it, and then drop back into a gentle ease with myself. I understand only in the contrast that the mad momentum of endless doing and its symptomatic emptiness is not how we are meant to live.

In complete solitude, I stop objectifying myself. In the bush I don't think of myself on some social hierarchy. I don't define my value as a comparison with others. The birds and animals don't judge me. It's a kind of healing in which I become human again. In complete solitude, we are not a concept of ourselves; we are ourselves.

It was St. Francis who said, "Wherever you go, preach the gospel; when necessary use words." Depicted as the only Christian saint looking down to the earth rather than upward to God, he has always held a deep appeal for me. It was St. Francis who gave up the life of a rich merchant's son that had been ordained for him and decided to go forth on a different trail and live simply in nature.

He is to me the first saintly tracker. Deeply connected to the wordless domain of animals and trees, and guided by a voice within, he lived a life of profound compassion. A compassion that did not need to be cultivated like some Buddhist practice, but rather a compassion that was innately present when he slipped the separating language of the mind and found himself in an unencumbered state of oneness.

Back on the tracks I will tell you the story now as the tracks are telling them to us.

The lion moved fast across the bare plain from the pan. For twenty minutes we followed in the soft sand. He was moving steadily when he suddenly cut down into a dry riverbed. Here he stopped. For a moment he sat down on his belly, his body and forelegs imprinted in the sand, flat soil farther back where his tail had lashed the earth. He then stood up and walked forward and then stopped again.

"This lion is listening," says Alex.

The forepaws left a deep mark in the soil as the lion had lifted his head, which hangs forward above the shoulders. The weight of the head traveling above the shoulders caused the forepaws to sink into the sand.

The track asks us questions. What did the lion hear that caused him to lift his head and listen? Another member of his pride? Or maybe it was prey. What is up ahead?

A narrative begins to emerge from the information conveyed by the tracks and by the set of hypotheses that the tracker begins to infer. Has he heard the sound of a kill up ahead? Has another male called wanting a fight? One must see the tracks and simultaneously imagine what the animal might be doing.

Our brains are hardwired to read these clues and make inferences. The mystery and danger, combined with problem solving, focus, and imagination, cause certain neural synaptic pathways to begin to fire. The result is addictively engaging. There is a neurochemical hit that comes with tracking, something akin to a runner's high. I have often thought that if people the world over could track on weekends it might spell the death of golf and soccer and mountain biking. We are a species that belongs within stories. We are the meaning-making animal. Tracking is a narrative that can help us reimagine why we are here.

Back on the trail now, I stare down the dry riverbed framed by the still presence of huge ebony trees. The imprint of the lion's body in the soft sand is two of my strides nose to tail. He stands. And then as told by paws exploding into thick river sand, he begins to run toward the unknown.

5

RESTORATION

For the next 3 miles, we walk just faster than is
comfortable. The soft sand follows a trail of explosive
holes left by weighty paws as the lion bounded down the
dry riverbed.

Only yesterday, I was on another continent in another
life and yet here back on my feet I feel myself anew. I am
reaching inside myself for something that I can't quite
land on that feels important. There is an alertness in me
that I haven't felt for months. My mind swirls through
a catalog of my life up to this moment, through all the
moments of destiny that put me here on this trail, on
this day.

The morning light filters through the thick canopy of
trees in sharp blades. Kudu and impala dart away from us
in flashes of white and rust as we walk.

Renias stops suddenly. Our feet crunch in the soft sand. "Yigesela," he says. *Listen*.

The sound of a toothy handsaw in a plank of wood. *Ha-he ha-he ha-he*. A leopard calls, no more than a mile away.

Alex and Ren look at each other. A decision not to divert toward the leopard passes silently between them.

"Tsika ingwe lesh. *Leave that leopard*," says Ren.

I'm surprised that the call is so close and yet Renias is not distracted by it. It's hard to know when to stay on a trail and when to divert. It's hard to know when the lesson is to persist and when the lesson is to let it go.

I think of all the angst I have felt between choices. I've been paralyzed by options and the idea that there is a single right way. Ren is more Zen; for him the only choice is the one he has made. He knows any choice will set something in motion. This is the magic of the bush and life. You use your intention, take action, and let go. The bush teaches us that the lesson is more about discovery than being correct. On the trail there is not one way; the only mistake is to not make any choice. As it is in life.

We continue on our path, and somewhere close by, the leopard continues on his.

It's 8 a.m., and having awakened before dawn, I have the sense that I have lived double the life of a normal day.

I feel a faint prickle of sweat and the reassuring weight of my tracking club in my hand.

The lion's trail suddenly turns. It cuts up a steep section of the riverbank.

We follow the obscure sandy explosion, a telltale sign of paws slipping on the steep bank, and just before the lion crests the top of the incline, I feel a surge of excitement as I see a perfect paw print. We are on the track!

The geometry of the lion's track as he powered up the bank is beautiful. An imprint of his essential presence in the world. A fleeting mark of wildness made all the more beautiful by the way it will fade back into untouched earth.

We crest the top of the bank and the land opens into low-slung acacia. I am struck by how I have walked on this land all my life but have never been to this exact spot. I have not exited the riverbed right at this juncture to see this section of ground. I get the distinct feeling that the lion is leading me. That he is trying to show me something.

Somewhere deep within a voice whispers, "I don't know where I'm going but I know exactly how to get there."

The wild self knows what you were meant to do. The wild self is whispering.

I track Renias as he walks, and I notice a faint shift in

his carriage and movement. In a strange way, I can see that whatever is happening to his energy is beginning to pull Alex in with it. They are starting to shift gears.

The process is somewhere between an artist's unconventional way and an elite athlete's big-match temperament. There are days when Renias just cannot get excited about a trail. But now, he goes into a zone. I can't say why this track is calling him to life or if instead he is bringing the track to life. Is he calling to it or is it calling him?

Renias moves into a deeper state of this power through presence. He isn't trying to do anything. By being himself, free from roles, rules, obligations, he is in a state of complete naturalness. Lao Tzu said in his ancient text the Tao Te Ching, "When nothing is done, nothing is left undone." I suspect he was pointing to this state of completeness, when one is absolutely present in life. The mastery is that there is no trying.

One ventures off the edge of the map here. There is no prescribed route, yet we know this place when we see it. We can feel it in great dancers and innovators and athletes. Yogis have spoken about it for thousands of years. It is as if Renias can feel what wants to happen. He is so deeply in the now that it contains all time.

Alex looks at me and for a second his eyes widen as if to say *Here we go*.

Renias flies along the trail, seeing what to most is invisible. Alex is close to him.

If the trail shifts one way, Alex will be on it. If it shifts the other, Renias has it. Hand signals fire between them. They are entering a state that to me, someone who has worked in countless leadership and personal development seminars, is what one might describe as a "leadership zone." They communicate seamlessly with each other. They are absolutely committed to achieving the goal before them, but that commitment hasn't become a burden. There is a joy to the concentration. Their eyes are shining in excitement. The task itself is generating energy. You could say they are playing on the track. The goal is not a fixed thing but a living creature. Perhaps this is always the highest pursuit of the trail: aliveness itself. Now, in my observation, I feel myself fall even deeper into the metaphorical; the metatrack for our species is to return to the trail of life.

The lion was walking on a bearing through the bush. Renias sees the tracks and then sets course on the vector, picking up confirmation signs as he walks. At the same time, he uses the trees up ahead as waypoints to orient himself to the geometry of the lion's trajectory. You must understand that what he is seeing is not large pugmarks in soft sand, but rather parts of the track. A bit of toe, a tiered back pad, some compressed soil, a place where some grass has been picked up by the compression of the lion's foot and moved somewhere else, leaving a shadow of where the grass had lain in the soil. Renias's brain is seeing the nearly imperceptible shapes that years of practice have taught him to see.

"If you want to learn to track lions you must track barefoot," Renias has said to me. He knows lions are inclined to walk on open thornless ground. He can anticipate where the lion will walk based on the foliage and the terrain ahead.

The landscape is beautiful, and as the masters find a new gear, I realize that the story of this moment is contained in a larger story. One that has shaped me and motivated me and is still asking to be told in a way I don't quite know how to say. Maybe this story is asking to be lived.

The past is coming to me now and I know it has something to do with this track we are on. If this moment in my life were the living line of a trail, could I track back to defining junctures? The track of this lion is informing the track of my life. My family's past. This place. This day. I feel myself in the place that Renias touches where all things are happening simultaneously in the flat circle of time.

My great-grandfather bought the land we now walk on

in 1926 after sipping heavily on gin and tonic at a tennis party in Johannesburg. The land was a bankrupt, scrub-covered cattle farm, gameless except for the lions that had ravaged the cattle. My great-grandfather, an avid lion hunter, decided while drunk with a friend and against all good counsel that they would buy it.

For three generations my family came here to hunt lions. They lived rough in the bush for the winter months during which they would track and shoot. My father shot his first lion at age fifteen, a year before his father died. In the grief of loss and under strong advisement to sell the derelict farm, my father and uncle decided instead to keep it. They made it pay by launching a shambles of a safari operation, which limped along until the arrival of Ken Tinley.

Ken was a high school dropout who got himself admitted to university by drawing a picture of a moth in such intricate detail that the dean of the faculty admitted him to the biological sciences department. After university, he worked in KwaZulu-Natal province on a groundbreaking conservation project to save the rhino. He then went to a reserve in Mozambique where he worked on a PhD to map the ancient waterways of the reserve. During his time living alone in Mozambique, Tinley developed a profound relationship with the landscape. He sketched the flow of water across the land and connected the movement of water to soil types and flora, which in turn informed the distribution of animals. He learned how to bring a wild place into his being so deeply that he could feel the landscape inside himself.

He lived close to the land in small fly camps and felt the deep connection of all things running through him as he became a part of that wilderness. Tinley's relationship with the landscape was spiritual, a state of being that occurs to anyone who lives in a wild place for long enough. It was as if there were no outlines of flesh to divide him from the ground and streams and mountains. The scientist in him was replaced by something closer to a priest or prophet. Then, civil war broke out in Mozambique and he was forced to run for his life.

Eventually Tinley made it back to South Africa and ended up around a small fire on a desolate property adjacent to Kruger National Park where two boys were trying to get a safari lodge going.

Ken, tall and good-looking in a Clint Eastwood kind of way, began to preach to them around the fire. For two boys who had just lost their father, he must have come as masculine directive manna from heaven.

"If you want this place to work, you must partner with the land and begin to think of the animals as your kin," he instructed.

"Partner with the land? How do we do that?" my father asked.

"Well, I will show you!" Ken shouted.

And there by the fire, a track opened before I was even born that would deeply shape me. Who is the maker of these trails of life? Threads across generations, threads between people, threads that most people never realize the effect of.

So many things had to happen for me to be here today. What compelled my great-grandfather to buy this land? What had made my father start a safari business against all sense? How had Ken come to that fire? My whole life I have been afflicted and blessed with a sense that there is a way in which life delivers us to a place ordered by some intelligence beyond our own.

I have often wished I could track back to those moments and ask those men, "Why did you do it? How do we know our destiny when we see it? How do we learn to track our life path?" The wild self is wise in a different way. Surely this is the deepest truth of a tracker.

The men I admired made choices against all convention and rationale. They followed something deep within.

They tracked what called and opened new trails of transformation.

There is a steady heat beginning to climb. The cool of the morning will soon be gone. My shoes are covered in a powdery dust and the sky is an endless blue. A small bush plane flies over us.

"Mgedeze, I hope this lion doesn't walk all the way to the Kruger Park," says Alex.

"Unga vileli," says Renias. *Don't worry.* "Hi ta swi kuma." *We will get.*

There is a smell of dung in the air and suddenly Renias whistles. "Tinghala ti lava ku hlota." *This lion wants to kill.*

The lion's tracks tee onto the tracks of a herd of buffalo. The ground has been churned by twelve hundred hooves attached to three hundred dark bovine shapes moving across the landscape like a slouching river of dust, leaving in their wake swaths of chewed grass and an aura of flies.

At 1,800 pounds and with sharp horns, the cape buffalo is a fierce opponent for a lion, and there exists between them an ancient rivalry, one that has seen lions gored and tossed on sharp horns and buffalo paralyzed with deadly bites to the spine. When you watch what a large black mane can do to a buffalo, you understand your own pathetic chance against a lion in a new way.

As paradoxical as it sounds, going down a
path and not finding a track is part
of finding the track . . . The path of
not here is part of the path
of here.

"Langota xiendla yini? *Look, what's it doing?*" This is a very Shangaan way of making a statement with a question. Instead of saying *Look what's happening!* the Shangaan language is more of an invitation than a directive. *Look. What's going on?*

Ren is standing over flattened soil and a pile of fresh buffalo dung. "Animals are clever," he says.

"You see, chap, this lion is covering himself in dung!" says Alex.

"He might be masking his scent," says Ren.

To me there is something beautiful about the image of this menacing killing machine pasting himself with dung like a sniper applying camouflage. The ground tells us the story of a lion that is now on the hunt.

6

LOSING THE TRACK

I once asked a great spiritual teacher if she had had a guru. She looked at me for a long moment and said, "My teacher was the desert and in the desert, everything is as it is."

As a tracker, I know what she means, for in the bush everything has its own natural way. The lion we are following is hunting buffalo. It is his way. When we search for the tracks of leopards we do so in shaded groves, not open savannah, because secrets are part of the leopard's way. When we follow trails, we become ourselves in the quest. The natural world, like a great Zen roshi, is profoundly impartial. It meets life as it is without judgments or assumptions or wishes for something different. It is at one with itself.

There is an intelligence that runs through things. To be a tracker is to be aligned with that intelligence. Carl

Jung referred to "synchronicity" as a simultaneous co-arising of something in the outer world with something deeply meaningful to your inner life. The place in space and time where your non-local spiritual self, vast and un-hindered, meets your human self in a moment of meaning specific to you. It is the moment when, in telling someone about a dream you had in which a beetle landed on you, a beetle flies in the open window and lands on you. It is a kind of glimpse into an order and meaning that runs beneath the face of reality; life winking at you. I suspect the wild part of you is at one with nature by being at one with the nature inside you. If you can unite these two aspects of nature, your own purpose is aligned with a greater purpose.

The land begins to rise into an open clearing spotted with great marula trees. As I am having the thought of living toward a different way, we enter the marula veld and Renias reaches down and puts a marula pip in his pocket. My thoughts and this lion's trail bring me here to this specific moment to see Renias do this. The simple action of reaching down and scooping the pip sparks a branching of meaning-making; associations, images, and stories arise inside me.

There is a genius to the marula tree. At certain times of year, the tree swells with juicy yellow fruit that elephants, baboons, and humans flock to eat. This cultivation of energy has a wisdom to it, the alchemy of turning nutrients from the earth into sugars, the use of those sugars to create a fruit that is tart and delicious at a time of year when there is no other fruit to eat. In this way, the tree disperses itself, ensuring its survival and evolution.

To live in nature is to watch the genius of this living technology unfold on the tilt of earth called seasons and to ask yourself, If this intelligence runs through all things, why not me? Who would I be at my most natural? How does a body heal or a person fall in love or a soldier make a choice to give up his life to save another's? In the moment with no social conditioning, who am I? If we are to become trackers, all of us need to ask ourselves: Trackers of what? New ways of living? A new set of metrics of what a successful life actually is? Can we, with the eyes of a tracker, see deeply into life and our own being and recognize a trail of intricately connected happenstance on which we know to move forward toward a new, more connected experience of life?

I don't know where I'm going, but I know exactly how to get there, whispers the wild self. *Learn to be natural.*

After hours of walking, we find the lion's trail has suddenly run cold.

There is a last track and then it's gone. Trails can be like life in that way. One minute you are clear on a path and the next instant, it is gone. You get fired, you lose a loved one, the company fails, you retire, she dumps you, you get divorced. Where you thought you were going vanishes. Who you thought you were is lost.

The ground has hardened and the herd of buffalo has scuffed it with so many marks that trying to find the correct track is impossible.

Alex and Renias change modes. Their twenty years in the bush have created a seamless cohesion. More than any other part of tracking, losing the track might be the most metaphorically rich. The tracker's next moves are an embodied set of instructions. Like an interpretive dance. Watching them move, I decipher a code of instructions for when you lose the trail:

Accept that losing the track is part of tracking.

Go back to the last clear track. There is information there.

Walk up ahead checking any open terrain and bare ground.

Open your focus.

Any place you don't find a track is not wasted, but part of refining where to look.

Flow for a while on your best guess, alert, listening, noticing.

Alex cuts back to the last track while Renias moves forward, zigzagging like radar sweeping the terrain. He checks any patch of open ground, the whole time maintaining a steady banter of "Hi ta swi kuma." *We will get.*

Once when just the two of us were out and and had lost the trail, Alex looked at me with his naughty smile and said, "Chap, often when I lose a track I just pretend to be Renias." We had walked forward, supremely confident, imitating Renias's gait, and found the track.

Alex refreshes the lion's last line of direction from the last track and moves forward, looking for clues and confirmation. The sun is higher in the sky and makes the light flat. Tracks with no shadow are hard to see. One hundred yards from the last track, in a pile of buffalo dung, Alex sees a single pugmark squelched into the buffalo pat. It is all the confirmation he needs.

And then the trail goes invisible again. Again, Alex vectors a direction.

I think of all the people I have spoken to who have said, "When I know exactly what the next thing is, I will make a move." I think of all the people whom I have taught to track who froze when they lost the track, wanting to be certain of the right path forward before they would move. Trackers try things. The tracker on a lost track enters a process of rediscovery that is fluid. He relies on a process of elimination, inquiry, confirmation; a process of discovery and feedback. He enters a ritual of focused attention. As paradoxical as it sounds, going down a path and not finding a track is part of finding the track. Alex and Renias call this "the path of not here." No action is considered a waste, and the key is to keep moving, readjusting, welcoming feedback. The path of not here is part of the path of here.

Coaching, I have learned, is just a kind of inner tracking. And it often begins when people have lost the track. It is learning a different way of moving out of a lost or stuck place. In its simplest form, coaching begins by asking a person, "How does that make you feel?"

"Terrible," they often reply, and then the coach says, "Well, then don't do it." This seemingly ridiculous statement can cause seismic shifts in people. We have become so unnatural and patterned and socialized that some of us don't even know what feels good or bad. We operate on autopilot. We are in our lives, but we are not alive.

The core of coaching does have a powerful central premise: your beliefs about life are not reality. A great coach asks you to question your deeply held beliefs and rules for yourself. You can go only as far into the experience of creating life as the limits of your personal belief system will allow.

I am astounded by the simplicity of this. Track what makes you feel good and bring more of it into your life. Notice what makes you feel lousy and do less of it.

When you say this to people, they either get it or they scream back at you. "You can't do that! You can't just do what you want!" Often, they fear that if they had the freedom to do what they wanted, they would end up on a beach somewhere, wallowing in excess and frivolity. They might for a while, but if they kept tracking, something deeper would start to express itself. When I see people actually track the desire in themselves, so often what they find is a desire to serve or be creative or share themselves in some way. But it is different for everyone. I once saw an artist realize he was tired of being poor and really just wanted a stable job with a regular income.

It is now hot. We walk on the trail of the buffalo, certain that the lion is still following them but with no clear sign of his tracks. Renias and Alex trust their hypothesis. They are willing to keep moving forward into the day, not on a track, but on faith. The light is flattening the earth as the sun ratchets itself higher into the African sky, making tracks harder to see. My shirt is sweaty and I find my concentration and desire waning.

Renias is a formidable walker. His thick forearms swing at his waist and I can see his concentration is conditioned. He is scanning the ground, listening, attuned even now as the trail has dissipated. He cannot let his mind drift. His focus is absolute.

"Let's just push forward a bit. I'm sure we will get something up ahead," says Alex.

He stops and circles something incredibly obscure on the ground. He whistles.

Renias comes back to look at what Alex has seen. After a brief glance he shakes his head.

"That's not it," he says.

I have come to learn that losing the track is not the end of the trail, but rather a space of preparation. The whole process is contained here as a pure potentiality. *Prepare yourself to hear the call, invite the unknown, look for the first track, tune in to the instrument of the body, and learn to see the track amidst many that brings you to life.* All of these dynamics must lie latent in you as you look for the next track.

It was out of the loss of a track that I found myself in my twenties working in the personal transformation field. I met a superb coach, Dr. Martha Beck, who invited me to travel with her all over the United States to attend her workshops in a loose apprenticeship. We had met a year or two before at Londolozi when I was still a safari guide. The year before that, I had been physically attacked twice. The first by people in Johannesburg and later by a crocodile. The second attack had left my leg mangled and me in a severe state of PTSD.

I was, at that time, all set to become a conservationist, in line with my family legacy. And although working, I often felt completely lost. And then one day, I had one of those deep moments of recognition.

Martha had come to Londolozi to go on safari with her family, and I was their guide. What I remember most about meeting her was that she articulated something I had intuited but didn't have the language for. "The restoration of the planet will come out of a profound shift in human consciousness," she said. "And that journey begins in the healing of individuals. Nothing is more healing than the realization and expression of your gifts. That's what I do. I help people find their gifts."

I was so struck by what she said that I felt my train go off its rails. A new track appeared. Martha said these words to me while we were driving through the restored landscape of the reserve. The moment felt orchestrated by some divine force — the outer landscape and my inner path suddenly infusing each other with meaning.

The restoration of the planet begins in people, the restoration of the planet begins in you, whispered the wild self.

It's a rare thing to have an encounter with your destiny, but as a tracker I had learned that it doesn't have to be. To live as a tracker is to know your track when it passes you. I knew mine when I saw it. I knew the truth of Martha's words, the feeling of expansion in my body. She was the first inner tracker I had ever met.

With that, everything collapsed. All of my ideas about what my life would be and who I was. What became solely important was learning what she knew.

A few months later, I found myself in the United States learning the tools of life coaching and how to guide a person back to his or her own inner guidance.

At the time, I had thought I was a life coach in training. But a few years in, the track cut a right angle in an unexpected direction toward another one of the best trackers I would ever meet, a shaman from the jungles of Peru called Rodrigo.

Rodrigo traveled the world working in the old ways of indigenous ceremony as a means to help people remember a different way of being in the world. In some deep way, the ceremonial spaces he made were places that taught people how to return to a more natural way of being. They acted as containers that tore away our conditioned layers of defense, social patterning, and emotional blocks so that people could experience, sometimes for the first time, the truth of who they were.

Slowly under Rodrigo's guidance, I learned to track a trauma pattern. How to see its signature in the way the body carries it, to notice things about a person that tell their untold story: the set of their eyes, the texture of muscle, their tone of voice. All of these things conveyed information. Working in ceremony was very much like tracking in the bush. All the signs were there in the room if you knew what to look for. If you could track a trauma pattern you could help a person find the self beneath the pattern. And there was a way of being with people who were scarred or flighty or aggressive that was like being with an animal. A way of being communicated in presence.

For ten years I worked intensely between ceremonial spaces and traditional coaching. Everywhere I went, I had a simple intention: help people heal in order to find their way back to their own guidance. And during this time, I was changing too. A very strange calling was emerging in me. The deeply held ideals about what I should be were giving way to an experience of myself. I could never have imagined that this was where my path would take me, but I knew I was on a trail following a track: the track of the wild self inside me.

I discovered my gift was to be with people in a way that could help them move toward a more authentic version of themselves. I was at the fringe, for sure, but I felt a tremendous fullness in what I was doing. It felt deeply fulfilling and important to me. To my surprise, compensation was coming with it. The more in tune I got with my calling, the more I found people willing to pay me to be with them. I saw very deeply how I could travel around remaking my home. I saw how healing perpetuates itself. My life as a safari guide had given way to a different type of guiding.

In all of these experiences, I felt my ties back to Africa. Away from home, I would think of Londolozi and be astounded by how a place can go into your being.

If you have never left a place, you may never know how deeply it has gone into your cells. Only in its absence, a world away in another land, would you hear its song calling back to you, playing the music of your longing. For me it was not just the magnetism of the African landscape that lived in me, but more deeply, the feeling of a land restored.

—

Back when Ken Tinley arrived on the scene, most of the land was eye-high scrub. The animals were scarce, and if you did see them, they were trying to get away from you, conditioned by years of hunting to escape the death that humans represented. A landscape, like a person or a psyche, learns to defend itself. With hundreds of cattle on the land, the grass had been overgrazed, leaving bare soil. When the rain came, the water would run off and cut deep erosive furrows into the earth. The arid landscape could not receive the nourishment it needed. I saw this too in every ceremony I attended, how trauma keeps a person from connecting with what they most need. And I recognized it in myself.

As the ground went into shock, it sent up scrub, and slowly that scrub encroached on the grassland until it was so thick that nothing could move in it. When my family had first arrived, they had thought that this was simply the way the land was. If something is all you have ever known, you mistakenly believe that's just how it is. Perhaps this is the greatest danger, that we don't even recognize another way.

This was why Ken was such a lightning bolt. Ken was a tracker of landscape, and he could see tracks no one else

could. He saw a whole other landscape waiting to be realized under the thick mat of defensive scrub. He saw a
wild beautiful garden that could be brought back to its
original harmony. Something about his intense confidence compelled my father and uncle to follow the trail
he was blazing.

"Restore the micro catchments! Plug the headward
erosion! Think of the land as your partner!" Ken bellowed
around the fires.

They rented an old bulldozer and began to smash up
the scrub.

"This is utter destruction," my father said when he
looked at the land after a day of clearing scrub.

"Trust me," Ken said. "Trust the process. It's not gonna
look pretty, but allow nature time to respond."

Slowly, methodically, they cleared the scrub away and
packed it into the erosive furrows. It stabilized the furrows
so the water no longer ran off, and this allowed it to be absorbed by the ground. That groundwater replenished the
parched earth and something miraculous started to happen: the pattern of the landscape was changing.

The grasses came back and the scrub no longer grew.
In the new grasslands, animals started to appear. My father to this day cannot contain the joy of those days as they
watched the animals return. Herds of zebra and wildebeest

began to flock onto the scrubless terrain. Rhinos walked into the open grassland. And herds of impala grazed in the evening light. The land was becoming itself again.

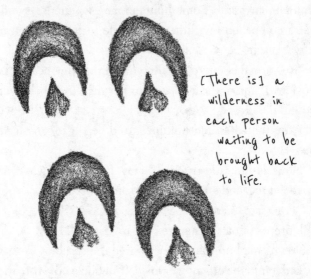

[There is] a wilderness in each person waiting to be brought back to life.

As a young boy, I had watched this transformation, not yet understanding that the land healing would touch my life so deeply and inform my destiny so profoundly. I remember the smell of the soil where a bulldozer had smashed the scrub and I remember thinking the land would never recover. I remember that same place a year later teeming with game. There was a sense that the land was grateful and that the animals could sense a change in intention and became calmer. With the sudden arrival of all these animals, the safari business started to do better. People from all over the world flowed toward this healing. The landscape had an energy and a vibrancy of antelope, insects, and birds. And then the wild cats we had once hunted started to allow themselves to be seen.

Now I was finding that landscape in every act of healing I was involved in. The restoration lived inside each one of us. When I looked at a person who was suffering or uncertain or lost or seeking, what I saw was a landscape. I believed that, like Ken, I had to look for what was there that was not yet realized. Through the eyes of a tracker I saw a wilderness in each person waiting to be brought back to life.

The restoration of the planet will come out of a profound shift in human consciousness.

As I traveled all over America, coaching people, conducting ceremonies, and creating spaces for people to rediscover the wild natural part of themselves, I felt myself walking through the landscape of my home thousands of miles away. It may sound strange, but the work of restoring the land that I had seen growing up was happening in ways I could not have imagined inside individuals all over the world who were answering the call to heal, to go wild again. If we were all a part of this great unfolding, then one person's peace was a deeper peace for all. If one person could become more natural, then that was a naturalness for everyone. In nature we learn that we are all connected even if we have forgotten that kind of belonging. The implications of this are profound. If it is true that we are one great being, then inside each of us is the chance for a different world.

Alex, Renias, and I would not be on this lion's track if not for the restoration. A landscape that is natural shapes all kinds of experiences. It gives of its abundance freely, like a person who has learned to be himself. As I walk, I am walking with my father and with Ken. I am walking inside their vision to restore the natural world, and I see how this land also is a place inside each of us.

My career had come to life and yet I still felt there was something more I was meant to do. It had been an incredible learning journey and it all began when I lost the track, as we had again now. On my lost trail, possibilities I had never considered opened up. A childhood in the bush and a life around campfire stories became an unexpected asset in ceremonial spaces around America. My lost track turned to first tracks and then trails.

—

I don't know where I'm going but I know exactly how to get there.

Now I see Renias in front of me walking with complete focus. I too am looking for something. I am looking for a lion. I am looking for my next track. The beast is moving out ahead of me, deep in his own wildness, deep in the story of this day. He is to us unrealized in form, yet his presence lingers in the spaces through which he has traveled. Even now as we walk forward on faith, with not a track in sight to guide us, we feel his imprint in our being.

His imprint is aliveness. His imprint is desire. His imprint is the mechanism that compels us toward mystery. Long before we have found him, he is answering my questions about how to live.

A song drifts into consciousness. A song from the earth asking to be deciphered by all those who have ever longed to find what they are looking for. Listen now, in stillness, underneath the uncertainty and rage and desolation. You may hear its lilting call in the longing of your heart. This is the song of the tracker.

7

BATELEUR IN THE SKY

High in a tree, a furred brute of a baboon is sitting with his legs tucked under himself and his hands resting on his knees.

Renias can't contain himself when he sees the baboon. Something about the incredible irreverent humanness of the way he sits hits a deep vein in Ren's sense of humor. He laughs slowly and deeply. He must have seen thousands of baboons sitting in just this way, and yet each time it brings him to a shaking mirth, as does the somewhat jaunty trot of a waterbuck, and any time a skulking hyena gets bitten by another and howls with almost theatrical oppression. Ren is endlessly tickled by these personality traits and characteristics. As a safari guide I had been taught not to anthropomorphize. The clinical eye of the scientific observer should not project human characteristics onto the animals. What isolation not to see our trickery in the jackal or the courage of a mother in a lioness around her cubs. As a tracker I wanted to take off the eyes of the superior impartial observer so the animals could inhabit me. I wanted to step toward kinship, not science.

"Languta mfen xi fana munu! *Look at that baboon! They are like people.*" He laughs.

Alex and Renias exist in my mind almost as an extension of one another. Over the years, Alex has tapped into Renias's humor and mannerisms. He often conveys a story to me that Renias has told him, complete with imitations of Renias's imitations. In the East there is a term for the way one can merge with a teacher, called "darshan." It refers to absorbing the teacher's spiritual energy and embodying it for yourself.

When I look at them together, I see something ancient like that. Over thousands of days in the bush together, a transmission has taken place. Not something that can be learned in books, but a way of being, a way of thinking and moving and seeing, that can occur only with time and presence. In truth it is the only way to learn. Often Renias can't tell you why he does something. He gets lost trying to explain. The deepest lessons must be lived.

The wild self, the part that is in touch with instinct and needs and purpose, the part that can feel shades of emotion and is natural, is like that. It must be awakened, followed, listened for—tracked. Men and women search for intimacy, but what they really need is wildness. A person who is in touch with the wild self answers a partner's questions in aliveness and presence—a different, more vital kind of conversation.

On one occasion when we had lost a trail, Renias walked us a mile up a dusty track and then cut at a right angle into the bush, where he landed perfectly back onto the trail we had lost. There was clearly some method to how he had cut off the road where he had, but he couldn't articulate why. It was just the nature of his experience, and at some point this had become a sense beyond language. The only way to learn it was to be near him so that over time his approach might become your own.

One day Renias will go to the other side, and so much knowledge will go with him. I know Alex feels the pain of this inside him sharply. "We have to find a way to preserve indigenous knowledge," he told me one night as we sat by the fire. His relationship with Renias has given him a pathway into an indigenous art form that is being lost the world over. We can't afford to lose the old ways, for in them live clues to a forgotten harmony and wholeness. They are the skills that can help us remember ourselves and the intimate belonging of all things. They help us remember how to be human.

When Renias imitates people and animals, they come to life before us, as they do with many great trackers. He is a tremendous mimic, and Alex and I have on occasion fallen down laughing as Renias morphed into the living caricature of an angry safari lodge manager, a French safari-goer with stiff legs, and then suddenly a copulating mouse that he had seen in the rafters above his bed. Renias can awaken the mundane with his sheer inner openness.

This ease is something I have often contemplated in my time with him, as it is something I have not seen in many people. I believe it has something to do with the fact that for trackers, no two days are the same. Once Alex took Renias on his first-ever plane trip from South Africa to London. The entire flight Renias refused to watch movies. Rather he stared at the sky map intently, watching the flight path of the plane. Upon landing ten hours later, he turned to Alex and, supremely content, declared, "Alex, if we need to walk home, I know the way."

We have crossed the threshold from tracking into just walking.

The trail of the buffalo herd shreds the ground, but the lion has grown wings. The track has lost its mysterious magnetism. Now we need Renias's mirth and ability to transform the mundane.

The sun is nearing the center of the sky and warthogs

garden vigorously on bended knees, snouts troweling the earth for the roots of winter grasses. A lilac-breasted roller flashes across the sky in a sharp blue arc. Slowly the midmorning haze settles in.

In the shade of an acacia tree, two rhinos sleep like discarded tanks, the odd ear flapping small puffs of dust at the base of wet nostrils.

A long way out, a bird cuts the sky.

You can't think your way to a calling . . .
You have to learn how your body speaks. You
have to learn how you know what you know.
You have to follow the inner tracks of your
feelings, sensations, and instincts, the integrity
and truth that are deeper than ideas
about what you should do.

Renias is the one who sees the bateleur eagle, named for the French word for "acrobat" because it appears to balance on an invisible rope as it flies. Suddenly, the bird's undercarriage appears, and it drops as faintly as a falling eyelash to the earth.

"Uxi vonile ximhungwe? *Did you see that bateleur?*" he asks.

Alex and I look up from the earth.

"When a bateleur drops from the sky like that it means maybe the lions have killed a buffalo or maybe, maybe, maybe the buffalo give birth to, to a calf." Renias's excited English can often develop a stutter.

From miles away, while examining the ground intently for the lost trail, Renias has managed to spot a falling eagle at an intense distance. So often we dichotomize between big-picture thinkers and details people. What Native Americans used to call "eagle vision" and "mouse vision." Trackers embody both ways of seeing. They move seamlessly between these two states.

"Let's get there!" says Alex. His blue eyes light up with new fire.

On a trail, something like this feels like a clue, a break in the case. A sign!

A jolt of energy flows back into me. I watch now as the

men try to pinpoint where the bird dropped in the wood-land ahead. We walk with renewed vigor and a sense of being back on track.

"Hi ta swi kuma," says Renias. *We will get.*

The internal GPS is intensely tested now as we close in on where we perceive the bird to have dropped. With a sense of horizon, this task is fairly easy, but as soon as we enter the dense woodland where we must weave through trees and still maintain a sense of where the eagle fell, the task becomes much harder.

There are still signs of the herd of buffalo as the sub-strate changes to islands of white sand surrounded by thick grass and towering leadwoods. A gardenia is flow-ering. Its pale yellow blossoms invite bees from far and wide. With the change in terrain, again the story takes a turn.

We cut the tracks of the male lion, and then suddenly the tracks of a lioness appear. And then a second. And then a third. Tracks on top of tracks. They tell the story of the lions reuniting and greeting each other. Walking closely together, they rub up against each other, their pugmarks overlapping. The pride reunited.

Renias sees wedges cut out of the earth where a small herd of zebra had suddenly accelerated.

"Maybe the zebra are running running from the lion,"

It's hard to know when to stay on a trail and when to divert.

he says. Sometimes one can tell where the predators went by moving in the opposite direction of the prey.

The lions walked together. A small wild band of cats that live day in and day out in the wilderness. Like a special forces unit, they must defend themselves; they must catch prey that has spent thousands of years of evolving to survive. They must protect their young and defend their territory. There is no fat in nature. Everything exists on the limits of its necessary entropy. The lions rest when it's time to rest, bond at times to bond, kill when it's time to kill, fight when it's time to fight. As a pride they are a unit with superb role clarity and discipline.

I have often spent an afternoon with a pride watching

them from a safari truck and then gone home as night falls and a fierce Lowveld thunderstorm rolls in. As blades of lightning smash down and the thunder goes nuclear, I have lain in bed thinking the lions are out there in the storm. There is no coming home to shelter. That is wildness.

The tracks of the pride suddenly diverge. The pattern of movement changes from a general direction to sudden irregular movement. Each lion moves in a different direction.

Renias whistles. "Tinghala xi lava ku hlota." *These lions want to kill.*

The change in the patterns of movement tells the story of a hunt. Lions are most dangerous on two occasions: when they have cubs and when they have meat. Something in them is activated when the air is thick with the smell of blood and flesh. Aroused by the instinct to feed, they can become aggressive toward each other and toward intruders.

When I was a young man, my father instructed me in how to handle a lion that was mauling a man. "Run in close," he said. "A lion will ignore you if it's mauling someone. Run in close and try to put the barrel of your rifle right against the lion and try to shoot it off the person being mauled."

Now armed only with the experience of the men I am

with and a small wooden knobkerrie, I walk on the trail of the hunters. The story is dense now with meaning and symbol. The trail of buffalo, a falling eagle, a pride reunited.

I am walking in a vision. I am walking in a dream. I am tracking. I am awake.

8

REMAINS OF THE FEAST

The great Zulu nation is a tribe that revolution-ized warfare in South Africa with the implementation of a strategy that involved speed, devastating weapons, and a tactic known as the "horns of the buffalo." Their infantry, fit and eager for a fight, would advance on the opposing army at a full run. Meanwhile they would throw two un-seen phalanxes, made up of hundreds of men, at a distance so far as to be unobserved. The horns would flank and then enclose the opposition without their knowledge. As the fighting began, the center would advance and be en-gaged and then, suddenly, the horns would appear on ei-ther side and the opposition would have a terrible moment as they realized they were surrounded and would now be slaughtered.

I have often wondered if the great military king Shaka

Zulu, who developed the "horns of the buffalo," did so as a result of his knowledge of how lions hunt.

The tracks tell this story in two lionesses that have split and set off in opposite directions. They are the horns. The male and another female have continued to move directly ahead. Their trail splits as they move apart to broaden the center of the attack. Without a single verbal word between them, the lions set the trap. Armed with devastating speed and sharp weaponry, they move like taut shadows through the grass.

The terrain changes into thick grassland. Rather than each of us following a trail, we stay together and follow a single path. The grass thickens into a brown mat. The tracks are difficult to see. We move forward on grains of sand and blades of grass. As the lion lifted its feet, sand clung to the pads and deposited on the grass as he stepped. To notice these things is work that sets the brain into a deep concentration, and I am struck again by how well-conditioned Renias's focus is.

It is a conditioning that comes out of a hard childhood. In the way that prizefighters don't come from rich neighborhoods, trackers rarely come from cushy backgrounds. The whole enterprise has to be accompanied by resilience, focus, and the dynamics of motivation.

When Renias was a boy his father owned cows that it was Renias's job to attend to. When he was only ten, he spent hours in the bush shepherding the cows, protecting them from lions, eating only what he could catch. A lost cow meant a savage beating from his father. A cow killed by a lion meant Renias would have to go after the lion and kill it. This was the life of a hunter-gatherer. This was life in the bush.

Being on the tracks of a pride that is now hunting awakens certain internal voices in me. The bush is thickening and I feel an element of danger enter more crisply into the fray. Everything in modern life seems to be about security. We are constantly sold our own fears. We strive for security, but at what cost?

Renias gives the hand signal for tracks lost, and now we have choices. Should we try to refind the track? Should we continue toward our best guess of where the eagle went down?

"You see this grass, chap?" says Alex, shaking his head. Dead grass lies matted on the ground in a kind of mulch that makes the tracks almost impossible to see.

"Where do you think that eagle went down?" I ask.

Almost as an answer, Renias begins to move in that direction. The bush becomes steadily thicker. With it comes a subtle kind of claustrophobia. I had been badly charged by a male lion in brush like this, and for days afterward, the event played on repeat in my mind, like a looping movie projected somewhere behind my eyes.

It was one of the first times I had successfully tracked a lion alone. I had moved on the trail, which ran down a powdery game path. I was seeing the tracks easily and moving fast. It was a path hippos used to enter a large water hole. I remember feeling deeply pleased with myself. Then, I looked up and saw the lion on top of a termite mound. The distance between us was less than 10 yards. He was watching me.

The first thing I remember is the look on the lion's face. The energy of it reached out and slapped my pleased face. The lion's tail lashed in irritation. He stood. Standing atop the mound, he looked giant. His gaze was locked on me. I felt my heart redline, my knees bend, and all of my internal voices scream "Stand!" The wrong reaction now could easily result in my getting eaten.

The lion began to growl and come fast down the mound toward me. His body conveyed with absolute clarity how dangerous he was. His eyes bore into my soul looking for weakness. I was afraid, but then something truer rose up above the fear. It was almost a kind of clarity of character

Everything in the
natural world knows how
to be itself.

that had been buried way down under all kinds of neuroses about my own inadequacy. Things happened so fast after that.

The lion ran at me. I shouted and returned his aggression. He bounded closer, then stopped and shot in the opposite direction, leaving me standing alone, shaking and pale.

I backed out of the brush slowly, my legs mushy.

In the days after the incident, I dreamed of that lion. I began to feel our encounter, although brief, was a kind of gift. To this day I wonder about the courage I found underneath the fear. I wonder if I could find it again. I wonder if it is wrong to look for it. I know that one of the great dangers of my life would be to live without danger. In our encounters with the edges, we come to know ourselves more deeply. Neurosis is a substitute for real suffering. Fearfulness is the most common state in a life that asks for no real courage.

It is with calculation that I move now deeper into the thicket. I look for the edges of what is sensible. I know that there is no room for egotistic bravado in the bush, and yet I do not want that edge to be my limit. I know that fear has something to teach me.

Of course, Renias's and Alex's experience makes a huge difference. Out here, surrounded by trees and the presence of wild beasts, we are a human community of three. Individuals made more by our trinity. People help each other grow through shared endeavor. I am traveling miles beyond where I could go alone. Alex has gone beyond where he could go, and Renias has had his life opened because of us. True giving gives in every direction.

Tracks of a hyena imprint the earth, the claws thrown into the soil by a bounding gait. The hyena stops suddenly and then turns to run in the opposite direction. The hyena may have run in toward the smell of meat and then turned to run upon seeing the male lion. The plot thickens.

At 60 yards, the eagle flies up out of thick grass and swoops low into a knobthorn tree. Ren looks to the eagle's crop for a bulge of meat.

We approach with caution. My eyes scan every patch of shade, half expecting lions to stand up out of the long grass. Yet there is no sign of them. Our sign has rendered nothing but matted brown grass.

Alex and I pace in larger and larger circles, hoping to find a track or a mark.

Everything is silent except for the sound of our own feet. In the thicket the air becomes suffocatingly still. The rim of my hat drips with sweat. I crinkle my eyes against the harshness of the light.

Renias is still wearing his jersey, as if he is immune to heat. He rarely drinks water, and I flash back to him saying, "Any pain, you can fix with walking. Just walk, you can be fine."

Tracking does not happen like it does in the movies. Butch Cassidy and the Sundance Kid are trailed nonstop by the Native American tracker despite their best efforts to elude him. The American tracker Tom Brown talks of silver lines through the forest that the mystical tracker can learn to see. In truth, while a trail can flow under the eye of a master, it is often a process of nonlinear problem solving. The story never goes like you want it to. The eagle is not the sign you thought it was. The lions start hunting and split up. The track runs cold.

Renias is standing still. He is contemplating. The eagle in this part of the story should have rendered something. Renias is rearranging all the clues in his mind. He is taking a moment. And because he is standing still, he sees flies zipping past him, all in the same direction. *Zzzzeeeooow zeeeeow zzeeeow.*

Slowly, he closes in on their flight path. The tracker is now stalking flies. He lifts his head and begins to sniff the invisible scentscape. He swings his head in the still air, sniffing out a carcass. Like a cartoon mouse on the wafting scent of cheese, he closes in on a grove of trees and the scene of the killing. The sign was not wrong!

The ground is still damp with blood and the stomach contents of a young buffalo. All that remains are hooves and a small pair of horns. The grass has been flattened down from where the pride fed.

"That's a burp in the wilderness," says Alex of the buffalo calf's fate.

Renias performs a rapid calculation. He looks at the horns of the animal to assess its size. I imagine him recalling the configuration of the pride as told by the tracks, a large male and three females. Then, he adds to the equation: his knowledge of lion behavior tells him that the big male would have dominated the small carcass. He feels the sun on his skin, knowing that the same heat would be touching the lions' skin. He judges the time of the kill by the wetness of the earth and the speed at which the blood might dry. I feel a thirst in my own throat and bend down to pick up a stone to suck on.

All of this information is run through his bank of experience. The story takes further shape.

"These lions are not full. A full belly would have driven them to instant sleep," he says.

"This is a small calf, they didn't eat much and now it's hot and I'm sure they want to drink."

The tracker reimagines the hypothesis based on new evidence. He then does what scientists who have studied tracking call "speculative deductive tracking."

He uses his knowledge of the area to throw a kind of tracking Hail Mary. From where we stand in the thicket, the closest water lies some 2 miles away—a river and the deep shade of mahogany trees.

"Let's go to the river," says Alex.

"I think the river is right," says Renias, always consultative in his ways.

We walk to the edges of the sandveld thicket. I am pleased when it opens into a sloping clearing and the land falls down toward the green finger of the river. Beyond it a series of koppies rises out of the earth as if some titan had built small oddly shaped towers with boulders.

To the east, the land runs for hundreds of miles of pure uncharted wilderness.

Looking out toward it from the high ground, I feel the space enter me and expand me in some fundamental way. The scope of the horizon liberates my imagination. Staring daily at screens, we have lost what a far horizon does to the spirit. As I amble behind my two mentors, dwarfed by the landscape, I realize they are living inside a different mythology. They are living a different story.

For thousands of years, to be outside the dominant cultural story spelled death. To be outside the band of hunter-gatherers meant you had been shunned by the village. Deep inside, we want to belong. This remains true today, but maybe for the first time in human history, modern society — the dominant culture — has become the thing that isolates us. If you could track your way out of the burdens of modern life and create an existence that is much more an expression of who you are, then your own life could become a living mythology. One that could inspire others.

Inside me I hear the wild self whisper, *Live it into reality.*

It takes some time to get down to the shaded banks of the river. A fish eagle calls, and somewhere in the middle of the reeds a hippo lets out his honking song of the African river.

The river is a dense green band of reclinata palms and thick reed beds. The band of vegetation is at least a mile wide and the stream runs through its center, over sand and white granite. The thick cool terrain is perfect for buffalo and leopards. The bank is scarred by the trails of herds of elephants and hippos making their way to the water.

Track awareness is how attuned you are to what is around you. It is recognizing a track when it appears. It is teaching yourself how to see what is important to you.

Along the upper section of the bank, a beautiful game path runs, well trodden by all manner of creatures as they move into groves of shade in the heat of the day. A band of vervet monkeys scampers away into low branches with our arrival.

We turn onto the riverbank and begin to make our way downstream. The path we are on will serve as a band of open sand that a lion print could be cut on. If they came to the river, this path would be the place to see a track.

I'm grateful for the shade of the huge trees that cling to the bank, and a southern boubou calls its metallic song. Walking on a game path is to the artistic part of myself a chance to see my own track laid down on the earth. My own step represented as a story in the earth. "The miracle is not walking on the water; the miracle is walking on the earth," said the teacher Thích Nhất Hạnh. "The miracle is all around us as the awareness of life itself."

"Hey mgedeze, are you checking out your clubfoot there?" asks Alex. "It sticks out quite badly!"

He and Renias laugh.

My right foot is a horrible rogue, thanks to a croc that nearly chewed it off at the river. Alex finds this truly funny. To look at my own tracks is to see something of my own being reflected in the gait. One straight print and one that sticks out to the right as if at any time it could go off in any strange tangential direction. The cosmic humor is not lost on me: that with a passion for tracking, a process that is literally about staring at the ground, I have at times struggled to be grounded.

We walk in single file. The bank is thick, but not nearly as thick as the riverbed below. Quite suddenly, there is a sound like a huge wet piece of canvas slapping against a studio wall. Through the branches of trees and scrub, down the game path, I can see the thick wrinkled skin of an elephant, black with wet mud. He shines in the sunshine. The elephant is walking down the path toward us, and although at a distance, I can hear the soft compression of his feet on the game path.

Track what makes you feel good
  and bring more of it into
your life. Notice what makes
  you feel lousy and do
less of it.

Renias kicks the dirt and a puff of dust rises and drifts on the breeze. We step in the direction of the dust, putting ourselves downwind. A few yards off the path is a small date palm. We move toward it and crouch down behind it.

The elephant is a big bull. His tusks shine white against the black of his wet body and he moves with a stoned sensuality. From the ground his size is overwhelming, and it feels to me as if his body is holding a deep vibration that charges the air around him. A sense of awe precedes him.

He comes so close to us that I can hear clods of mud fall off him and land on the ground. I can smell on him a combination of crushed vegetation and fermenting leaves. I can see his eyelashes and the way the cartilage of his foot gently expands as he steps. From time to time, his ears flap and the gallons of blood in them are cooled before heading back to his heart. He stops and sniffs our tracks.

He becomes aware not of where we are, but that we have been there. He lifts his huge head and slowly looks around. A bull like this might have walked deep into Mozambique and raided village maize fields there. Poachers may have shot at him or equally he may have had few encounters with humans in his lifetime. I believe that elephants hold some old wisdom in the core of their being. I watch his giant trunk sniff the air. I see Alex's excited grin next to me. We are very close and it brings an almost silly elation. I feel light-headed. We are one field of life dancing in many forms.

The elephant breathes in deeply and then shudders. He swings his vast head and moves forward. As the elephant walks off, I can feel his presence fade like the waning vibrations of a huge gong. I feel full.

In truth I am done. I could go home now and be happy. I hear Joseph Campbell: "People are not looking for the meaning of life, they are looking for the feeling of being alive." If that was it, I had found it.

When I set off this morning I could not have known to expect this moment. The life of a tracker is made astounding because of moments like these. Life on the trail will bring you into contact with so much unexpected wonder.

As if reading my thoughts, Renias and Alex turn their attention back to the lions. "Let's push on!" they say.

9

ENTERING THE ZONE

The game path is now compressed with the wrinkled tracks of the elephant. As large as steering wheels, his feet on the earth have wiped the path clean of any other tracks. Shining clods of mud sit in a trail where he moved.

The sound of the river as it runs over rock and sand and the gnarled roots of matumi trees that grow at the water's edge is a faint melody telling the story of the water's journey from the escarpment of eastern South Africa down into the Lowveld and then onward through the emptiness of Kruger National Park and on to the flat floodplains of Mozambique, where at some forgotten estuary it will greet the sea.

As it runs its course it wordlessly creates life. In the villages, women draw water in large buckets and young boys fish for bream and barbel. Inside the reserve, the river offers water on hot days for giraffes; it provides reeds and nest sites for thousands of birds. It invites huge trees to its richly soiled banks, and it asks for nothing as it gives life out of its very riverness. All around us, nature quietly teaches of abundance.

Down the trail we persist, hoping that the tracks of thirsty lions will cut across the game path as they journey to drink at the water's edge. Renias walks at the front, then Alex, then me.

We are entering our seventh hour on the trail, and I find myself inside a time paradox that occurs in the bush. The distinct feeling that we have been out either for a few minutes or for days.

I'm terribly thirsty now and wish that I could go and dip my face in the river, but I am conscious of not wanting to seem weak. As I look at Alex and Renias, it appears that in six hours of walking, of intense focus and vigilance, and with no food or water, they have not broken a sweat. It is a kind of energy I have witnessed in people who have merged "work," "mission," and "meaning." These people don't take holidays or need days off. They outwork everyone not from some kind of gritty determination, but from a place of pure pleasure.

"Chap, we need a track here," says Alex.

"Don't worry," says Renias. "I'm sure they will come here. I know these lions."

Renias is a student of the patterns of animal movement. Years of tracking particular prides in the bush means he often knows a favorite trail or crossing point in a ravine. He knows the particular tracks of particular animals and their individual personalities.

Then, there it is. A beautiful pugmark. One of the lionesses in the center of a crinkled elephant track.

To live as a tracker is to know your track when it passes you.

"That's proper art," says Alex.

The elation of returning to the track is hard to articulate. Dopamine floods the system. The break in the case! The clue that changes everything!

Down the path, more tracks. The pride all together. The tracks of females and then over them, the larger

tracks of the male. Full from eating the bulk of the carcass, he walks well behind them, laying his trail last. The
tracks are on top of the elephant's and the elephant passed
only a short time ago. This tells of a freshness that truly
puts us in range.

Renias stops and turns to me. "Come, buti, it's your
turn now," he says.

He brings me to the front of the line and offers me the
trail. My job now will be to follow, and as we are close, Renias and Alex will look over the top of me into the brush
ahead so that we don't come upon the lions without seeing
them. At the head of the trail, I feel the natural pressure of
being thrown the ball in front of the people I admire.

Suddenly, I feel an old friend who has walked with me
for years arise. Each one of us has these friends; mine is
called self-doubt. I have learned rather than to resist him,
to invite him in, welcoming him as a teacher of humility.
Together, we continue. The first track, and then the next
first track.

I am rusty and my eye is out of practice. Even after
tracking all day, the pressure of being the lead jams me up.
I feel myself go out of my body and into my head. Everything becomes a question. *Is that a track? Is that? No, they
wouldn't walk there. Did they go the other way?*

"Yima, yima, buti. *Wait, wait, brother,*" says Renias. "Okaaay." Okaaay is usually the beginning of a pep talk.

"Okaaay, buti, I can see you thinking too much. Don't worry, we will help you, just try to enjoy yourself."

I start again, walking in staccato bursts. Track. Track. Track. I feel my eyes dusting off the rust of American life. Track.

Alex gives me a pointing hand as a kind of confirmation. "Good," says Renias.

The trail diverges into multiple paths, through a reed bed that has been cut knee-high by the heavy winter feeding of elephants. The game is to pick the right path as it diverges into many options.

My pace becomes less jerky and begins to harmonize with the pace of the lions. My focus sharpens. The tracks appear with more ease. I feel my body again and then the faint sensation of losing all sense of myself in a profound absorption. I am pulled forward by the almost alive energy of the trail.

Tracking is a doorway into a flow state. Flow is a psychological state defined as full engagement in a task. It is the place where the lions and the track and the tracker become one seamless unfolding. I feel my way into the first hints of that level of concentration now. I feel my pace increase and my focus deepen. Where the lions split, I pick the trail. My eyes scan the ground 10 to 15 yards ahead of me. Images of faint tracks, a lion's toe, a bit of back pad, sand on grass.

I am locked onto the trail, but my focus is wide-open. The trail is like a beautiful obsession. I feel drawn to it. I can feel the lions moving out ahead of me as if there is a cord of energy between us.

Upriver, a vervet monkey high in a tree sounds his alarm at the passing danger he sees in the river below. The lions. Then beyond him, a nyala barks its warning, then a squirrel chatters its alarm. All the animals are speaking of the danger moving in the river ahead of us. The track is telling a story on the ground. The animals are speaking of predators. It is all happening NOW.

So many questions in my life are unanswered, but now I feel myself on my path.

The field of life is guiding me, talking to me, leaving signs for me at every turn. The living stillness inside me takes control, and as it does, my self-consciousness and judgment fall away. This moment is complete and it contains perfectly all the moments that have been and all that will ever be.

I have followed the lions not to a place, but to a state of being. The experience is spiritual.

I fly along, feeling like my own feet have left the ground. Alex and Ren are in tow.

My body moves, my eyes decipher. All trying recedes into complete ease.

It is all here on this trail; this track is the realization of my purpose. There is a gift in the trail that reverberates into my future self. A gift given to me by the lions.

They have helped me remember the wild self that is alive in me — and in each of us — and called to a different way of being in the world. Every seemingly unconnected track has led here to this realization: my track is to send out the call to the tribe of forgotten trackers and ask them to remember.

A feeling full of information enters my body. In this trancelike state, the sensation speaks. The wild self knows. Just as when I first felt called to be a coach, I feel a similar feeling now. My destiny is evolving. I see a new trail opening.

Suddenly, the wild self that has whispered all day begins to speak boldly.

You who have longed for and felt called to make a different world. You who have suffered the illnesses of society. You who have risen to the top and found it empty. You with a desire to serve. You who have felt called to nature and to the creatures of the earth. You are the tracker.

We are now at an inflection point. We must leave the safety of the village and venture out onto the trail of something wild and uncertain and as yet undefined. We must live on that trail, propelled forward by a set of clues only you will recognize by the aliveness they bring out in you. You must teach yourself to see your track!

You are here to live. Your life can be the beginning of a great change; and it must be.

It was all there. My lifelong obsession with healing nature, the reason I grew up in a wilderness restored, my passion for tracking, my years traveling in ceremony, my desire to tell stories. All of these inclinations. All of these unexpected tracks of my purpose lined up into a simple task: tell the trackers all over the world it is time.

Let them track a great healing inside themselves. Let them track their purpose in the world. Let them find what restores them. Give them a new old way to think about their life. Let them track forward into a new mythology for the world to live inside.

A person who is living in the authentic wild self becomes a transformer. Not by what they do, but by the very realness of their life that asks others to switch on. In these times, an authentic life infused with meaning is a kind of activism.

Step off the superhighway of modern life and go quietly onto your own track. Go to a new trail where you can hear the whisper of your wild self in the echoes of the forest. Find the trail of something wild and dangerous and worthy of your fear and joy and focus. Live deeply on your own inner guidance.

There is nothing more healing than finding your gifts and sharing them.

In the sand ahead, a set of paw prints spins 180 degrees so that they face toward us. The prints are like a rock in a fast-flowing river, backing the flow of energy into an eddy on the trail. I hear the poet Rumi: "What you seek is seeking you."

As all the lions walked away, one female turned to look back down the game path toward us. Unable to hear or smell us, she has felt something deep in her instinctual body. At high levels of any art form, the practical gives way to the mystical.

I imagine that as I had realized my calling, she had

looked back to me. She had looked down the trail to the trackers. And then she moved on.

I emerge from what feels like another realm to see Alex and Renias walking close behind me. I am returning to this place with a new vision, and for a time Renias, Alex, and I move fluidly on the trail, leading and following in a shared state of flow. We are each the fingers of a single hand. Each connected to the same task. I feel the closeness in the center of my chest. If they are my friends, then I must be okay. If they are my brothers, then there is nowhere I can't go.

Ahead, the ripe sun drops lower into the afternoon haze. A waterbuck stands in utter stillness on the far bank.

My eyes follow the thread of lion track as far forward as they can: 10, 20, 30 yards ahead. "Throw your eyes forward," Alex used to tell me. Now I have thrown them forward to my purpose.

The bank cuts into a small ravine made by the nightly back and forth of huge-bodied hippos to the river. There the tracks of the lions slide in the damp mud as they turn off the bank and head into the deeply vegetated reclinata palms that make up the body of the riverbed. Down there, the only means of moving is to crawl through the dark tunnels of dense palm fronds. Down there, it is thick, and the sound of white water renders the ears useless. Down there, buffalo sleep. Down there is where the lions have gone.

The three of us stand on the edge of the bank and look down into the ravine to the tunnels beyond that open like the mouth of a great green beast. We know there are monsters down there. We have reached the moment that asks us about our commitment, our motivation, and our madness.

There is a beat of hesitation. We look at each other. Then Renias steps down the bank.

10

THE HIPPO TUNNELS

It is the magic hour. The light is now "the light that makes everything beautiful," as the Shangaan call it.

The bark of the trees and shape of the leaves are etched in perfect detail by the clarity of the light. Nature watches silently as we disappear down the uneven trail that the hippos have cut into the bank.

The descent into the riverbed transitions us from the relative safety of the bank into the blind danger of the riverbed. But I am not concerned with safety. I know this trail is a part of my story and *I know to do this*. I feel attached to the guidance of the wild self.

I feel a solid sensation across my shoulders. I feel my feet welded to the earth.

This is how I feel when I'm living on purpose, I think. This is the track of my life manifest as emotions and sensation.

Going forward, I need to daily "do what I know to do." Not the rationale of fulfilling some role or image but the deeper knowing of the moment. I carry this feeling forward into the reeds. Soon the brush swallows us up. A breeze blows down the river, and the palm fronds rub together like crinkled paper. In the tunnels we crouch and move forward inch by inch. Thoughts of wartime tunneling run through my head. Salt sweat runs into my eyes. Occasionally, a tunnel opens, revealing the sky like a gasp of breath.

I can smell the lions in the soil. And then a huge male lion turd, still warm and pungent on the path. Renias points to it and gives the hand signal for very close.

We know we are close. The question is are the lions still moving in the center of the river where we will not see them or are they now sleeping somewhere in the thicket?

The tunnel opens onto a small beach. The thick river sand is full of the tracks of the pride as they spread out to drink at the water's edge. The male and then the tracks of the three females. I can see Renias looking closely.

"I think another female has joined," he says.

In the coarse river sand we see the tracks of a civet. A civet is a large catlike creature. The realization that follows is collective. This is not a civet track, but rather the track of a lion cub.

The discovery dawns on us in the sickeningly slow way that a mistake reveals itself. Renias begins to scan all around us. If we have put ourselves closer to the cubs than the mother, she will not take kindly to that.

It is like someone has turned up the voltage, and I feel so much adrenaline flood my system that the taste in my mouth changes. We know the lions are very near, but the arrival of the fourth lioness with her cubs changes the risk profile dramatically.

The closest Alex and Ren have ever come to being killed by a lioness was once when they had mistakenly gotten between her and her cub. Alex told me that initially she had run away from them, but then as she ran, he saw her front right leg flex and she pivoted and ran a tight half circle and came straight at them. She stopped less than a yard away, and Renias threw a small log at her. She pinned them there, threatening to leap forward at any moment, and the time that passed felt like a lifetime. Eventually she turned and left them. Alex vomited and they didn't speak about it again.

That type of situation in this terrain, where both humans and beast have no place to go, would mean extreme danger. Holding on to each other, we stay very still. Alex has a mad look on his face. He is enjoying this.

I can sense Renias feeling for the proximity of the lions. Slowly, we move back toward the tunnel that leads to the beach.

The bush is psychedelic with color. My hearing is electric. My sense of smell is capturing everything. The animal in me is fully awake. I am alive.

I emerge from the tunnels different from how I went in. More and more the message lands. We are a society that lives in denial of death and so we are a society that denies life. But out here, how flimsy we are, with no boundaries between us and nature. What a wonderful teacher of how to live. In the face of fear is also something like awe. Then after the awe, humility. Humility is the liberation from illusions of dominance, control, and power. I give up the importance of my life to instead become a part of life. Guided by the intelligence of the nature within me as it also unfolds all around me. This is an alignment with a deeper purpose, the feeling of being both great and small at the same time.

Back on the bank, we laugh a nervous laughter born of the release of tension. "Ngozi straight," says Renias. *Straight danger*.

Then slowly, he begins to move from tree to tree while staring down at the river.

Moments later we see them. On a small sandbank, in a clearing in the reeds, we see the pride. The beauty of their form, the wildness held in the shape of their bodies, is breathtaking. I feel myself connected to the mystery, suspended in the communal joyful consciousness of every tracker through the ages who followed and found what they were looking for.

From behind an ebony tree we watch them. The small cubs chew on their mother's ears. A few feet away, the male lies, staring down the river. The scene could be millions of years old. It is deeply comforting to witness. Our beautiful, wild teachers who have helped me find the trail within the trail.

There is nothing more healing than finding your gifts and sharing them.

We bump fists. "Aye, I like this," says Renias. Alex is smiling his cheeky grin. With sunburned arms and tired feet and a deep thirst, we radiate a simple joy of a day of tracking.

We are there to see it. We have told the lion's story as trackers and the track itself has helped us to tell our own.

I am glad to live in a world with the presence of lions. Even now as I write this, from the safe confines of my room, I know somewhere out there right now a lion is walking into a vast wilderness to live its secret life.

Alex radios in the position of the lions to all the guides who have guests on safari. In minutes and hours, they will come. The pride will be seen, and who knows what their beauty may ignite.

Alex and Ren watch for a few minutes, and then we turn to go.

It feels short to me, almost anticlimactic. But Ren and Alex were never motivated by the outcome. They live on the trail. And now, so do I.

EPILOGUE

In the weeks and months after that fateful day tracking the lion, I became obsessed with writing. In the last hours on the lion's trail, the next track for me became clear. It was exciting how all the seemingly unrelated tracks of my somewhat strange life — the land, the lions, the trackers, the guiding, the healing — converged in a moment into a clear path: to send out the call to others, to share what I had learned. I didn't know where I was going, but as it turned out, I knew exactly how to get there. This is the elegant intelligence of life.

I want this book to be a call to the tribe of forgotten trackers. Maybe you are one of us. It's time for us to track from a different center. As our first act of activism, we should track down outer lives that more closely reflect our inner values. We should reimagine our own lives into more meaningful expressions. This is a part of the great restoration that will begin in the life of individuals. To live as a tracker is how we take responsibility for transforming the planet. Imagine the effect that millions of people tracking from a different center could have on our dominant cultural story. The magic of the wild self is that each of us is guided in our own unique way, and yet together the process charts a new way of living for us all.

Alex and Renias, ever my guides, continue to show the way. With the support of the visionary South African philanthropist Gaynor Rupert, Alex and Ren were able to found the Tracker Academy to preserve indigenous knowledge. Using Londolozi as one of their training sites, they have begun to take applications from young men and women all over South Africa, including some of the poorest communities in the country. To date, they have trained hundreds of the most incredible and skilled young trackers, and the academy has a 99 percent placement rate into industries such as tourism and anti-poaching and animal studies.

When I look at these superb graduates from the academy, I see an ancient art form being preserved in these young men and women. And I see the gift of mentorship continuing to travel.

As if that weren't enough, Ren and Alex are now telling their stories on stages all over the world. Together they tell stories of tracking and the power of their relationship. To see Ren, a man who had been born under a tree, captivating thousands of people on an international stage is truly a sign of how, when we follow the inner tracks life has laid for us, we never know where they might lead.

As for me, I'd gone all over the world and then come home and realized that tracking, this art form that had been such a part of my life, contains all the lessons we need for transformation. I discovered that my calling is to send out the call to the trackers out there. My next track was tracking itself.

It became obvious that it was time to combine my two main passions — the African bushveld at Londolozi and guiding people toward their own inner navigation. I decided to create retreats that would take people out into the bushveld, experiential learning adventures in which people begin to learn the process of tracking the wild self inside.

Alex, Renias, and I teach people the old art form of tracking and give them a way to experience an inner parallel so that they can take it back to their life. For me, this work has been the culmination of a dream: all of my favorite things woven together. We didn't go out and get these jobs; we created them out of following the inner trail. We kept making our lives as trackers.

You can't study this at university. As trackers, we are literally feeling for what the wild self wants and then marking a trail into uncharted territory. Living as trackers, we feel into the work that is most important to us, and find our way to it. Yours will be different. It may need to be created, but if you use the skills of the tracker you will be pulled toward the life that is calling.

I remain deeply convinced that a person who tracks down an authentic life opens up possibilities for themselves, their family, and their larger community. In these times, as the planet screams at us to reimagine our way of life, these new possibilities are deeply important.

You must become a tracker and set out on the trail of your wild life. If you track your authentic life and uncover its meaning, it will catalyze other possibilities for living, and what's important to you will immediately change. Meaning doesn't want more; when you're in deep touch with your wild self, you know you have enough and are enough. From that place of enough, you act in service, because that's what feeds you. It's a lot of individuals going on that journey of discovery that will create transformation.

Remember to prepare for the call. Know the call when it comes by the fact that not doing it would feel profoundly wrong. Open yourself to the unknown. Develop your track awareness. Amidst all of the information that surrounds us, learn to see what is deeply important to you. Use the feelings in your body as a guide. Live on first tracks.

Anything that puts you into your essence, no matter how small, is valuable. Even if you don't know where it's going, play with it. Find friends to track with, lose the track, keep trying things, get feedback. Find your flow and remember to see how many unexpected things come into your life by living this way. It will be scary at times. Let the fear bring you to life. I suspect that if you give yourself the room to live each day as a tracker, a deep calling to serve will emerge.

So my friend, as you read this, let this be a call to you. It's time.

Go track.

ABOUT BOYD VARTY

Boyd Varty is a tracker, life coach, and storyteller. His vision to "track your life" engages audiences across the world on the subject of forging connections in ourselves, in our communities, and with the earth. He speaks to those who long for a way of interaction both simpler and more profound than the way most of us live in the world today. Boyd has a psychology degree from the University of South Africa. He is a certified Master Life Coach, the author of two books, and a TED speaker. He divides his time between his home in the South African wilderness and the United States. You can learn more at www.boydvarty.com.

ABOUT ALEX VAN DEN HEEVER
AND RENIAS MHLONGO

For the last twenty-three years, Alex and Renias have worked together conducting specialized safaris, training wildlife trackers, and sharing their inspirational presentation "The Power of Relationships" (www.motivational speaker.co.za). Their journey together has taken them from tracking leopards at Londolozi Game Reserve to following grizzly bears in Yellowstone National Park and speaking internationally. They have worked throughout Africa and around the world, including in Brazil, Peru, North America, the United Kingdom, and Australia.